KB107606

Theoretical Perspectives for the Public Sector and Its Agendas

Junmo Kim

머리말

행정학 분야 중 정책학 분야에 관련된 이론들은 사실 그 범위가 매우 넓다. 그렇다 보니, 정책학을 전공한 학자들 간에도 세부적으로는 전공 영역상, 방법론상의 차이가 매우 크다는 점에 놀라지 않을 수가 없다. 그러나, 학자들마다 취하고 있는 고유한 이론적 배경의 상이함에도 불구하고, 공통 영역으로서 공유되는 영역들이 있는데, 이 책에서는 이러한 공통 영역에서 자주 언급되는 이론들을 집약해 보고자 하였다.

즉, 계량적인 접근을 취하거나, 철학적인 접근법을 취한다 하더라도 정책의 논의를 위해선 지난 시기에 사회과학의 여러 분야에서 만들어지고 활용되어 온 이론들을 중심으로 정책과 정책학의 논의가 이루어지기 때문에 이러한 공유되는 공통 영역에 대한 이론들의 수요가 충분하다고 생각되었다.

이 책은 상당 기간 동안에 조금씩 준비된 원고들을 영문으로 모아서 단행본으로 만들게 되었고, 출판시기 등의 이슈로 국내 출판을 기획하게 되었다. 이러한 이 책의 기획 의도가 다양한 독자층에 속한 분들에게 여러모로 도움이 되시길 기대해 본다.

2023년 10월
저자

Preface

As a scholar in the field of Public Policy, it is a common and widely shared understanding that the field of Public Policy has been relying on multiple domains of theories and literature for its guiding lights both in academic pursuit and practical prescriptions.

With an intention to synthesize different streams of theories that I have been exposed, different series of books are in the process of publication. This book is one of the efforts mentioned, and especially focuses on descriptive theories used in Public Policy fields.

I do hope that this book can be a guiding light for someone who is in the pursuit of knowledge and theoretical endeavor in Public Policy fields.

October 2023

Junmo Kim

TO MY LORD JESUS CHRIST
WHO GAVE ME INSPIRATION

CONTENTS

Chapter 1 1
Introduction 1

Chapter 2 4
Theoretical Framework for the Public Sector 4
1. Theoretical Framework 6
2. Theory of Bureaucracy and Its Impacts on the Public
   Sector and Public Policy 70

Chapter 3 94
1. Current Status and Achievements towards Globalization
   96
2. Origins of dissatisfaction regarding the globalization of
   the Public Sector 101
3. Institutional Analysis and Its Contribution 114

Chapter 4 131
1. Prologue 131
2. The Old Paradigm 132
3. The New Paradigm 138

4. Paradigm shifts in social sciences ·························145
5. Concluding Remark ································154

Chapter 5 ································155
1. Prologue ································155
2. Traditional approach to Dual Use Technology
   Development ································157
3. Interdisplinary Approach to Dual Use Technology
   Development : A Background ························160

Chapter 6 ································171
1. Future for Communitarianism and liberalism ··········171
2. Policy Learning across nations and its policy
   implications ································174

Bibliography ································175

<Tables>

< Table 1> Factors of Social Capital ·······················109
< Table 2> Concept of interdisplinary research ·········167
< Table 3> Comparison of the notion of interdisplinary
          fields ···167

<Figures>

< Figure 1> Globalization and Gov't Performance ·······97

Chapter 1

Introduction

1. Background and Purpose

Theories related to Public Policy range from theories in economics, political science, management and business studies to economic geography, accounting, statistics, and philosophy. While this wide range is taken for granted, as an author and scholar, it was sensible to divide the literature into several theoretical areas. Following this line, my recent publication focused on Public Policy theories by focusing on decision and policy related parts ranging from agenda setting to policy making. In comparison, this book will cover more descriptive theories in their nature arising from political science and 'pure' public policy theories that are somewhat detached from quantitatively oriented theories and approaches.

No matter what scholarly stance a scholar takes, the

necessity to grasp the understanding of 'basic' public policy related theories will never cease away. By taking this as a backdrop, this book will usher different audience groups into a range of basic theories widely used in public policy studies.

2. Scope of the Book

Following chapter 1, which is the Introduction of the book, chapter 2 will present a wide range of theories in different schools of thought on the "process" side of public policy. In my view, in the landscape provided by the classical political theory, each subsequent theory brought its own structure and actors to make a more refined theoretical framework. After the classical theory, chapter 2 will introduce group theory, pluralism, and expand into a more modern theories like collective action theory, institutionalism of different intellectual traditions, followed by theories on Bureaucracy.

Chapter 3 will cover institutional analysis used in public policy in an applied context. Contributions of institutional analysis for policy transfers and institutional re-design is the title of the chapter reflecting the contents. After chapter3, chapter 4 will treat paradigm shifts in Social Sciences, which is an unique feature of the book. Chapter 5 will treat a policy case, followed by the conclusion chapter, which is chapter 6.

Chapter 2

Theoretical Framework for the Public Sector

Prologue

If public policy is defined as a collective level problem solving in the context of democratic institutions, a researcher can think of not only specific government programs, but also surrounding environments of these programs. Thus, the theory of public policy includes naturally theories explaining policy process and policy outcomes & alternatives. While theories on policy outcomes are mainly dominated by quantitative analysis, theories on policy process have been provided by the discipline of Political Science.

The "process" aspects bring us a pivotal question on how societal demands are articulated and processed through the state. It is possible, on this question, to start with a more fundamental idea on where does the state come from, and illuminate different theories on state-society relations framework.

In this chapter, I will review different schools of thought on the "process" side of public policy. In my view, in the landscape provided by the classical political theory, each subsequent theories brought its own structure and actors to make a more refined theoretical framework. Depending on different theories, different focal points were utilized with different advantages and disadvantages. Thus, in some theories, societal aspects of participation and representation are emphasized, while in statism, the state as an actor is more emphasized. In my view, different theories offer students of public policy with rich understanding of the policy environments as well as how theory development has been proceeded over time.

1.Theoretical Framework

1) Classical Political Theory

1.1 Setting the stage for state-society relations

Classical Political Theory seeks to provide an explanation for the origin of society and the state through the consensual action of the people, the social contract.

Contract theories have a common notion in their deductive theorizing that human beings were once living in a state of nature without government.[1] These individuals were rational beings, and therefore realized that their lives can be enhanced through the process of organizing a political society. Based on this political society, people established the government.

Despite these common grounds, different authors provided different understanding for the solution to the

---

1) Thomas Hobbes, *Leviathan,* chapter 13. Penguin Classics, 1992. p.185.
   John Locke, *The Second Treatise,* Broadview 2015. paragraph 19 and 91.

state of nature. In Hobbes, his reasoning is focused on why the state of nature is the state of war.[2] And then brings out his point that given his analysis of human nature, to halt the insecurities posed by the state of war ,in which everybody is against everybody, absolutism is the only answer to the problem caused by the state of nature.

For Hobbes, no alternative to the absolutist state can provide so stable a resolution to the problem of disorder, and no other alternative can guarantee the same degree of freedom from internal disorders and maximal response to external threats than absolutism. Based on this line of reasoning, for Hobbes, limited authority restricts the capacity of the sovereign to address the sources of conflict; also limited authority cannot provide enough assurance for people. Without assurance that others will conform, it is irrational to constrain one's own action.

Against Hobbes's "prescription" of the absolutist state, Locke's objection to it emphasizes that to create

---

2) Thomas Hobbes, *Leviathan*, chapter 13. Penguin Classics. pp.185-186.

an absolutist state is like being eaten by a lion, instead of escaping from pole cats and foxes.[3]

In Hobbesian contract, a collection of individuals comes together and form an association by agreeing to accept the authority of the sovereign(who governs them and who has the right to determine the rules of cooperation). Thereby, the social glue is their common subordination. In comparison, Locke's contract suggests a two stage approach to the problem of forming a political society.

In Locke's contract, individuals agree to form a separate commonwealth, i.e. to form a "People", or a "particular political society" distinct from the natural community of humankind.[4] In the second stage, the People establish a government by choosing a "form" of government or constitution. Thus, Locke thinks that there are more fundamental aspects than the bond of common submission to the authority of the government.

Furthermore, implicit in Locke is that people are

---

3) John Locke, *Two Treatises of Government*, The Second Treatise, Paragraph 93.
4) John Locke, *The Second Treatise*, paragraph 95-- 99., and 128.

considered as a corporate body or a unified agent that entrusts its sovereign authority to the government. Because of this conception, the People retain the right to judge whether trust is being kept or violated by the government.[5] This means the people can withdraw its "entrustment" in the case of the reconstitution of government.

1.2 Theoretical Contribution

From Hobbes, we find the state as an alternative to disorder, and at the same time, one can notice a seed for the Leviathan or the super state that chokes the liberty of people. Therefore, from Hobbes, we are faced with a dilemma in deciding the balance and extent the state's power and authority are justified. Following Hobbes's argument, his way of deducing his conclusion is more persuasive than his conclusion for the absolutist state, which denies the possibility of self-government.

In Locke, with a similar contractual setting, we find a possibility for self-government, and a check from

---

5) John Locke, *The Second Treatise,* Paragraph 149, and Paragraph 240.

societal forces on the government.

Among numerous contributions, it is possible to extract following points from the contract theories. First, the unchallenged beauty of the classical political theory is its normative and ahistorical nature. It is this nature that still sheds light on our political discussion of today. Second, from their initiation, subsequent academics could continue on elaborating theories from both societal and state sides. Third, more specifically, Hobbes's diagnosis and conclusion is exactly analogous to today's collective action problems. In this sense, Hobbes is a forerunner and a foundation for the rational choice theory which starts from rational individuals, and build up theories for collective action problems.

Fourth, these classical pieces raised a more fundamental quest for the prospect for democracy; is it possible to achieve a self government? or should we admit a pessimistic understanding of human beings?; i.e. human beings rational at individual level are irrational at collective level. These questions can always be validly raised at any subsequent theory development, although these questions do not appear on surface always, due to different treatment in diverse theories.

2) *Classical theory of Democracy*

While classical political theory has set a landscape in which state and society is established, and has provided room to be filled by subsequent discussion of the state-society issues, classical theory of democracy brings in "individuals" and their participation" in the landscape.

Classical theory of democracy has argued for the virtue and feasibility of direct participatory democracy. Ever since Rousseau who championed the classical theory on participation, the issue has never left the stages of state-society relations in public policy discussion. In this section, I will review the core arguments and theories of participatory democracy, its critics from modern political science literatures, and assessments on the two opposing views. Then, I will introduce a seed for a new stage of discussion on state-society relations, the groups, referring to Madisonian view.

2.1 Core Contents of Participatory Democracy Theory

Rousseau presents the functions and virtues of participation with several foundational assumptions that individuals, who are interdependent, have property and their economic differences are not so great to lead to political inequality. Rousseau also recognizes possible existence of "tacit associations" and argues that these tacit associations would not make an argument for a policy, and continues that there ought to be equal and numerous associations possible.

With these foundations, Rousseau builds his theory of participation. The key point to understand Rousseau's claim on participation lies on the relationship between the authority structure of institutions and psychological qualities & attitudes of individuals. The crucial variable is whether political institutions are participatory or not.[6] In the participatory settings, the main function of participation is an educative one. By educative function, Rousseau implies that people learn how to make collective decisions, harmonize a personal interest with collective decision, and doing so learn how to ensure freedom in a political society. Although Rousseau's arguments are made in the settings of city government, and critics are eager to point this out, proponents of the original Rousseau's position, including Mill, would argue that participation at the local level would be a "proving ground" for a larger, national level practice of participation that will ensure democracy. In this sense, despite Mill's disagreement with Rousseau on the equality among people, since Mill acknowledges elites' existence, both Rousseau and Mill have an optimistic belief on the educative function of participation.

Virtues of participation in Rousseau's world can be articulated in three core arguments. First, through participation, people learn private and public interests

---

6) Carole Pateman, *Participation and Democratic Theory*, Cambridge University Press, 1970. p.24.

arc linkcd through participatory decision making. The logic is as follows; a person learns that his fellow citizens will resist the policy and implementation of inequitable demands. Thus, he learns to distinguish his own impulses from public values, and knows how to be a public and private citizen at the same time. A consequence of this is to have a "good government, while protecting others' private interests. Another consequence is the increased freedom; it is because participation in decision making endows a person a degree of control on the political decisions.

The second function of participation is that participation makes individuals to accept collective decisions more easily, since they directly participated in the formulating process of the decisions.[7] The third function comes from an integration effect participation brings in. Following Rousseau's line of argument, once the participatory system is established, it is a self-sustaining system in which participation reinforces democracy.[8]

---

7) Pateman, op.cit. p.27
8) Pateman, op.cit. p.25.

J.S. Mill generally takes the core idea of Rousseau in his theory, except for a part where he adds his points on participation at the larger level polity. Despite this expansion, Mill still keeps the core elements in Rousseau, which tell us that participation at the local level teaches democracy to individuals. In theorizing, on the other hand, Mill seems to accept the inevitable nature of representation in the modern politics.[9]

2.2 Critiques on Classical Participatory Theory of Democracy

The core idea of critiques is denying the claimed educative function of participation, and arguing that more participation is not desirable. These critiques sprang from J. Schumpeter's idea on democracy.

Schumpeter presents a modern definition of the democratic method as follows; "institutional arrangement for arriving at political decisions".[10] Schumpeter

---

9) Pateman, op.cit. pp.30-31.
10) Joseph A. Schumpeter, *Capitalism, Socialism, and Democracy.* Harper Torchbooks, 1942, 1947. p.269.

introduces a market analogy into politics by comparing political competition for votes with the competition in market places. In this analogy, voters choose between "political solution packages" offered by politicians, and political parties act as regulators in the competition.

In Schumpeter's picture, the only participation is possible through voting for leaders. Thus, in Schumpeter's critique of participatory democracy, there is no central role of participation. Rather a focus is given to leaders.

Later scholars in Political Science have a common point with Schumpeter on the point that classical participatory democracy is questioned for its feasibility. Berelson points out that qualification of citizens is not met to fulfill the ideal of participatory democracy in the modern politics.[11] What is more striking from Berelson's point is the implication from the currently low political participation. Low political participation and apathy is the decisive factor that our current political system is in

---

11) Berelson, Bernard R., Paul F. Lazarsfeld, and William N. McPhee. Voting: A study of opinion formation in a presidential campaign. University of Chicago Press, 1954, 1986.p.307.

its stability[12]. It is directly opposing the view of Rousseau in which implicitly more participation is recommended.

Berelson, while reducing the status of participation, does not mention on what characteristics constitute a democratic nature to a political system. On this point, Dahl provides his clue. In presenting his clue, Dahl succeeds Schumpeter on following points. First, democracy is understood as a political method, and second, competition in electoral process is the democratic element in the political method.[13] In addition to his common points with Schumpeter, Dahl adds that modern democracy is a polyarchy, where there exists multiple centers of power.[14] Also political equality is redefined with a "proxy"--- the universal suffrage and equal access to a polity.

With this newly defined democracy, a consequence of an increased participation is a disastrous one. Dahl

12) Pateman, op.cit., p.7
    Berelson, op.cit. p.316.
13) Robert A. Dahl, *A Preface to Democratic Theory*, Chicago, University of Chicago Press. 1956. p.84.
14) Robert A Dahl(1956), op.cit. pp.133-134.

claims that since the lower socio economic status(SES) groups have authoritarian personalities, increased participation would bring destabilizing effects on the political system.[15] On this point, Satori also suggests a similar view; he claims that the active participation of the people in the political process would lead to totalitarianism.[16] Furthermore, Eckstein warns that at the national level the structure of authority is far from a purely democratic one.[17]

2.3 Assessment

(Validity of the critiques from the contemporary theory)

While the contemporary theory of democracy presented sharp criticisms, it may be reasonable to argue that authors of the contemporary theories regarded the classical participatory democratic theory as descriptive theories, while in fact these theories can be regarded as normative ones.[18]

---

15) Dahl(1956), op.cit.
16) Giovanni Satori, *Democratic Theory* Detroit, Wayne State University Press 1962. pp.135-148.
17) Pateman, op.cit. p.13.

At the same time, these contemporary theorists were replacing the normative contents of the classical theory with their own points. Implicitly and explicitly, the contemporary democracy theories supported the political system where representation takes the "seat" that was taken by "participation" in the classical democratic theory.

(The second round)

Despite the gloomy theoretical positions shadowed by modern political science, and macro sociological theories, a different research tradition presented a promising aspect for participatory democracy through education.

During the world war II period, a research was conducted to encourage consumption of specific parts of beef in preparation for the shortage of food, including liver.[19] In a psychological experiment, members of the American Red Cross were divided into 6 sub groups.

18) Pateman, op.cit. P.15.
19) Kurt Lewin, "Group Decisions and Social Change," In G.E. Swanson, T.M. Newcomb and E.L. Hartley, eds. *Readings in Social Psychology*, New York, Holt. 1952. pp.459-473.

Among these six groups, for three groups lectures were given on the nutrition information and the rationale for consuming the specific parts were introduced; for the remaining three groups, discussions were arranged by themselves on the identical subjects. The result was that in the discussion groups, 30% of people changed their attitude to cook the parts of beef they ordinarily do not consume, while in "lecture" group only 3% reported that they actually consumed the parts. An implication from this research was that discussion and education were functional to participation.

Another similar example is by John French and Lester Coch at an apparel factory; In their experiment, they knew that workers at a factory were fearful of the change in production methods, because it will require a new learning for them. The factory they researched had this problem, which often came out in a form of high turn over rates at the time of production method change. The purpose of the research was therefore how to ensure workers to stay, and at the same time introduce new technologies. For this, three groups were prepared: non-participation group, representative group, and full-participation group. The result showed that in the full-participation group, workers showed low turnover rates and higher productivity.[20] As Pateman mentions, the evidences show that not only participation has favorable effects on the individual in the sense that it brings political efficacy, but also participation at least does not undermine the efficacy of the system itself.[21] But there are caveats in this line of argument. In political science literatures, there are more theories that tell us about stratification and its effects on political participation.[22] This means that most of the theories support the arguments by the contemporary theories rather than classical theory of participation.

One methodological problem from the small scale "experimental studies" in finding macro political implication is as follows. Since these psychological experimentations were conducted in a "small group

---

20) Lester Coch and J.R.P. French, " Overcoming Resistance to Change," *Human Relations* Vol. 1.(1948). pp.512-533.
21) Pateman, op.cit. p.66.
22) Samuel P. Huntington, "The Democratic Distemper," *Public Interest*, no.41. Fall, 1975. pp.9-38.

setting", when a researcher attempts to bring the implication to a political context, the research is faced with a problem of changing the level of analysis; there is a jump in borrowing the results directly to a macro context. In addition, since the original purposes of these researches were more instrumental in nature,[23] questions can be raised on whether we can draw out an implication for democracy from the results.

Another criticism comes from an attitudinal study by John Goldthorpe.[24] According to him, contrary to a common expectation on the embrougoisement of working class, these people have not showed any change of attitudes; an implication drawn from this was a dismal picture for democracy through participation.

---

23) In French and Coch's research, the purpose of the study was to find a causal link between micro level productivity and participation; in Lewin's example, the purpose was to see whether attitudinal changes occur under participatory environments. But the research has a wartime background.
24) Goldthorpe, John H. The affluent worker in the class structure. Vol. 3. CUP Archive, 1969. Chapter 5.

3) Group Theory

From as early as Madison's and Tocqueville's analysis, we can trace the root of the role and nature of groups in Democracy. Madison regarded groups or factions as potentially harmful and therefore was proposing to incapacitate their effects through group competition.[25] Tocqueville also saw the dynamic of groups in American political landscape.[26] Truly, Madison had an insight and therefore could be regarded as a forerunner for the thought of pluralism, group politics, and cross-cutting nature of individuals and group membership.

In comparison with the previous part on classical doctrine of participation and representation in democracy where individuals are emphasized, there is a point to make to introduce the group in modern politics. The point is that in the modern democratic settings, in

---

25) Madison, James. "Federalist paper number 10." The Federalist Papers (1787): 23-33.
26) Tocqueville, Alexis de. "Democracy in america." Democracy: A Reader. Columbia University Press, 2016. 67-76.

addition to individual participation and representation, much of the political dynamics is carried out by groups that include interest groups and associations. Group theory, in this sense, illuminates a realistic understanding of modern politics in which groups take inevitable and essential roles, since Rousseau's theory of direct participatory democracy always leaves a question of feasibility in a larger scale.

Group theory is clearly a societal side theory in a dichotomy of state centered and society centered theories. It shows how societal demands are channeled into a polity. What group theorists have done in describing politics was eliminating the negative side of the group and emphasize the outcomes of group politics as desirable; this is a change of a mindset descended from Madisonian view.

In establishing a theory, group theorists have modeled their theory after economic metaphor of a market in which groups replace individuals and group outcomes substitute an equilibrium in the market.[27] The

27) Theodore Lowi, *The End of Liberalism*. The Second Republic of the United States. Second edition. W.W. Norton &

established theory was named as "pluralism". In this section, I will review the core elements of pluralism, and then discuss the implications for the balance between the state and society. More specifically, I will discuss two issues of the relationship between the state and society: representation and participation, and the nature of the state. In discussing the representation issue, I divide the issue into two: representation between individuals and groups, and then representation between groups and the state or a polity. With this schema, I will turn to a body of critics on pluralism.

3.1 Core contents of Pluralism

Pluralism is a theoretical approach that describes a way of transmitting preferences of societies to a polity or the state. The theory of pluralism was considered as a theoretical reference for describing American Politics in the post war period as well as a model of politics for pluralistic industrialism, which is the politics of the

---

Company. New York and London. 1979. p.22., P.35.

mature societies in the "convergence theories". Pluralism assumes the stability of the political system and efficiency of the outcomes of the group politics, given the settings of competing interests. Pivotal features of pluralism can be articulated as follows.

First, groups are considered as fundamental building blocks of a society. These groups are freely organized as intermediaries in a two way communications between the state as an arena and society.   Second, group affiliation largely determines individual attitude and behavior. Each individual is expected to have more than one affiliation, and therefore cross-cutting of membership helps to stabilize the political system.[28] Third, the state is regarded as an arena where competing interests articulate their interests.[29]   Fourth, pluralism assumes multiple centers of power in a society.[30] Thus, in pluralistic society, in each policy

---

28) Taylor, Michael, and Douglas Rae. "An analysis of crosscutting between political cleavages." Comparative Politics 1.4 (1969): 534-547. pp.538-546.
29) Lowi, op.cit. pp. 36-40.
30) Robert A. Dahl, *Who Governs?* New Haven Yale University Press 1961.
   Nelson Polsby, *Community Power and Political Theory*, New Haven Yale University Press. 1963.

arena, a small portion of population determines policies, depending on their interests. For pluralists, it is sufficient that ordinary people have opportunity to join the circus if they wish to do so; channels between voters and decision makers are open, but not always activated.[31] Fifth, pluralists argue that all legitimate interests are heard. David Truman's concept of "potential, latent "interests shows that any interest can be mobilized with low entry barriers. In this context, pluralists may argue that inequalities may exist, but are non-cumulative. With these pivotal features, politics is explained as partisan mutual adjustment process by interests.[32]

3.2 A Critical Analysis

As any theory does, pluralism has assumptions in its theory building. In this chapter, I will concentrate on

---

31) There are latent groups in Pluralist model, which can be activated depending on issues.

32) Charles E. Lindblom, *The Intelligence of Democracy* : Decision through Mutual Adjustment. The Free Press New York. Collier-Macmillan Limited. 1965. pp. 16-17., pp.153-162.

assumptions on the state, representation, and participation. When these assumptions fall either empirically or theoretically, then the persuasive power of the pluralist theory is reduced at least proportionally.

Assumptions in pluralism can be articulated briefly for a discussion purpose. First, pluralism assumes that any voice can be heard. Also, since groups are formed freely and naturally, there is no mis representation virtually. Second, multiplicity of power centers means elites do not overlap on different issue areas. Third, the state is an arena, and reduced to a status of an interest group.[33] Fourth, by pursuing interest group politics, the state is undermining its legitimacy at the same time the political system is endowing legitimacy to the outcomes of group politics. In the next part, I will provide a critical discussion of the assumptions to evaluate pluralism.

---

33) Lowi, op.cit, p.36.

3.2.1 State-Society issue I: Three issues on Representation and Participation

Since groups take the role of aggregating demands and interests from individuals, it is possible to formulate the structure of representation in pluralism in two stages: between individual and interest groups; and between interest groups and the policy making unit or the state.[34] With this structure and against the representation mechanism in pluralists' picture, there are at least three objections to refute it One point is on the pluralist' assumption that any voice can be heard. Mancur Olson shows why some interests can be mobilized, while some others cannot. The second objection is on the problem of representation: whether interest groups represent the people correctly. In other words, whether relationships of power within groups were organized to produce outcomes that served the

---

34) This is my suggestion to integrate different critiques on the pluralism's representation structure.

The State
|
interest group
|
individuals

interests of members. The third issue is on whether there are biases in representation between interest groups and the state.

(The first issue: The logic of Collective Action)

Mancur Olson offers an attack on the pluralist notion of the formation of interest groups and politics by suggesting a theory on how and under what conditions collective goods (political interests) can be provided with his analysis based on a metaphor borrowed from economics. Interest formation is viewed as a collective good, and individuals are assumed as rational actors. Furthermore, with rational individuals, the formation of interests depends on incentives to individuals, i.e. whether the interests can overcome free-rider problem or not determines the formation of interests.

In comparison with the pluralistic notion that any interest can be mobilized and organized in a society, in Olsonian world, only small groups and large groups that can supply selective incentives can be mobilized and maintained as interest organizations. In the pluralistic picture, it has been assumed that citizens with a common political interest would organize and promote the interest.[35] Latent interests are easily formed to protect their interests upon necessity. Furthermore, since each individual is engaged in more than one group, i.e. cross-cutting membership, a consequence is a vectoring of pressures of group competition, which leads to social stability. From this view, it is natural to state that if workers, farmers or consumers are faced with monopolies harmful to their interests, they would attain countervailing power through organizations such as labor unions or farm organizations.

In Olson's view, the pluralistic view is not so realistic, due to the "collective action problem", which stems from the nature of rational individuals. In a hypothetical collective action case, the very fact that the objective or interest is common to or shared by the group entails that the gain from any sacrifice an

---

35) Mancur Olson, *The Logic of Collective Action: Public Goods and the Theory of Groups*, Harvard University Press, 1965. p.112.

individual makes to serve this common purpose is shared with everyone in the group. So the individual in a large group with a common interest will reap only a minute share of the gains from whatever sacrifices the individual makes to achieve this common interest. In this context, from the notion of rational individuals, Olson draws the "free-rider" problem; no one will sacrifice, and hope to be a free rider. A consequence is no mobilization.

Olson argues that any large interest group needs selective incentives other than collective goods for their existence and maintenance. Union dues is an example of negative selective incentives, while American farm organizations usually offer positive selective incentives. From the above reasoning, Olson suggests following generalization: Under the assumption that other things being equal, the larger the number of individuals or firms under an association which would be benefiting from a collective good of a political interest, the smaller portions of the gain from action in the group interest will be allocated to each individual or a firm that undertakes the action. Thus, in the absence of selective incentives, the incentive for group action diminishes as group size increases, so that large groups are less able to act in their interest than small ones.

From Olson's critique, we can find deficiencies of a pluralistic assumption that any legitimate voice can be heard; with this assumption, pluralists would assume equal access of diverse interests to a political society. The beauty of his analysis comes from the point that he provided a generalizable hypothesis based on rationality assumption of individuals. In this sense, Olson is considered as a harbinger for the rational choice institutionalist approach that came later on in the scene of political analysis.

(The second representation issue: power within groups)

The second issue on representation deals with a following problem; whether relationships of power within groups were organized to produce outcomes that served the interests of members. Pluralists have been advocating the virtue of group representativeness for public policy, and at the same time denying Michel's law of oligarchy as not empirical. Samuel J. Eldersveld argues that the concepts and components of the "iron law" may not be applicable to the U.S political scene. Another encouraging result for pluralists was a research on the "Typographical Union" by Seymour Martin Lipset, which provided empirical evidence that in some organizations, organizational structure favored competition among leaders; thus, in this line of argument, the organizational structure provided members with resources for controlling outcomes, and thereby denying the law of oligarchy.[36]

Against this benign argument in favor of pluralism, there are arguments against it. Pizzorno argues that as interests are aggregated, their representative organizations tend to become bureaucratized. It is exactly a modern revival of Michels' law of oligarchy.[37] Charles Sabel

---

36) Seymour Martin Lipset, Martin A. Trow, and James S. Coleman, *Union Democracy*. The Internal Politics of the International Typographical Union. The Free Press. Glencoe, Illinois. 1956. pp.393-418.
37) Alessandro, Pizzorno. "Interests and parties in pluralism." Organizing interests in Western Europe. Cambridge University Press.1981. pp.247-284.

also provides similar results through his research on Italian labor unions. Thus, based on these researches, it is possible to question the representativeness of interest groups in the pluralists' picture of politics.

(The third issue: biases of representation between groups and the state) Arguments by Mills, Schattschneider, and Lowi

The third issue on representation is on whether there are biases in representation between groups and the state. On this issue, there are different critiques, while pluralist theory is silent on the issue.

One of the most prominent author in this critique is C Wright. Mills. In his book, The Power Elite(1956), he argued that the "command posts" in American society were dominated by three interlocking groups: political leaders who are generally declining in power; corporate leaders who joined the political directorate during the New Deal in the 1930s; and military leaders also joined.[38] He claimed that the wheels of communication between the

---

38) C Wright Mills, *Power Elite.* New York Oxford University Press 1956.

three groups are facilitated by their similar high status backgrounds. Mills, however, acknowledged that their interests would not necessarily converge.

A response from the pluralist camp reacted on Mill's criticism. Robert Dahl, in his influential study of New Haven(1961)[39], argued that in the city of New Haven, no single group pre-dominated across all policy areas, and their roles and kind of alternatives they had to choose were different. Dahl suggested that in order to establish and verify the existence of a ruling class or elite, one should examine a series of decisions where the preferences of the ruling elite insist what is counter to those of other groups. Dahl's main argument was that a careful scrutiny of key decisions in New Haven revealed no cohesive ruling elite, regardless of whatever local people say in their interviews on who has power in the region.

Pluralists' defense, such as Dahl's, looks persuasive, but still leaves insufficiency to draw full attention for a following reason. That is, an influential study in New

---

39) Dahl, *Who Governs ?.* Democracy and Power in an American City. New Haven . Yale University Press.

Haven cannot be sufficient ground to repudiate the argument for the existence for the ruling elite. Furthermore, Mills arguments were succeeded by neo-Marxist theories, in which the state is an instrument of the ruling class, as in instrumental Marxism. Similarly, in the functionalist Marxist view, the state, with its autonomy, exercises its power in favor of the capitalist class.[40]

In comparison with Mills' argument, Schattschneider claims following points.[41] First, private interest groups are the best developed, and most active groups, which are dominated by business interests. In comparison, in voluntary associations, there is a strong upper class bias. Second, political parties, by extending the scope of conflict, are not captive of special interests; since they can find counterweights in the society.

These authors, Mills and Schattschneider, have a common point in that they observed "biases" in

---

40) James O'Connor, *The Fiscal Crisis of the State* New York. ST. Martin's Press. 1973. pp.1-30.
41) Schattschneider, Elmer E. "I960. The semi-sovereign people." A Realist View of Democracy in America. The Dryden Press, 1968.

representation. Mills interpreted the bias through a "class structure" perspective that there exists a ruling class, while Schattscneider saw the upper class oriented pressure politics that alienated "ordinary people".

In relation with this common thread, Theodore Lowi's criticism is a more refined version of the Plural Elitist theory. A subtle, qualitative difference with the two authors is that in Lowi, the government is captured by interest groups.[42] In my view, Lowi's understanding and criticism of representation structure in pluralism is more persuasive. Lowi shows that the development and advent of the interest group liberalism coincides with socio-economic development. In common with what James A. Morone says, economic expansion made laissez-faire policy incapable of dealing with more complex issues. If we extract core ideas of Lowi and Morone on the socio-economic conditions for the pluralism, what was actually forged out of the changing socioeconomic situation was the expansion of

---

42) Lowi, op.cit. pp.57-60.
  Martin Lodge (ed.) et al., The Oxford Handbook of Classics in Public Policy and Administration chapter 16. pp. 221–234. Oxford University Press 2016.

government in a way to create specialized bureaucracies to match 1: 1 with organized interests.[43] Also during the New Deal, it was encouraged to form representative organized interests to perform economic policies. This allowed and facilitated interest groups to capture the government agencies.[44] Another compelling reason to accept Lowi's criticism is, even though one denies the existence of the ruling class, Lowi's argument allows a room to accommodate politicians and organized interests' in the log-rolling. [45]

3.2.2. State-Society issue II: A consequence of Pluralism:

According to Pluralists, political outcomes, or the outcomes of the group politics, are always desirable, and lead to an equilibrium, which is a metaphor from economics. In addition to the virtue of desirable outcomes, pluralists also claim that the outcomes are

43) James A. Morone, The Democratic Wish: Popular Participation and the Limits of American Government. Basic Books, A Division of Harper and Collins Publishers.1990., p.122.
44) Morone, op.cit. p.133.
   Lowi, op.cit. pp.58-60.
45) Lowi, op.cit. p. 55.

efficient, given diverse interests competing for support. For example, Charles E. Lindblom justifies, with a market-borrowed analogy, the political outcomes of pluralism in the name of "partisan mutual adjustment".[46] It is, however, a subject of an empirical scrutiny whether the equilibrium is really working.

Authors like Pizzorno warns that the pluralist system of representation is inherently unstable.[47]Pluralism, according to him, tends to undergo a cyclical emergence of new collective identities on the scene or the recurrent explosion of ideological passions. This dovetails with Lowi's analysis of interest group liberalism, in which politicians could reduce burdens of political solutions by transferring the burden to group politics outcomes.[48] To be clearer, while at the group level, when interest representation becomes bureaucratized, and those bureaucratized interests compete for their policies, the political consequences of that would be "uncontrollable explosion of demands and ideological passions for

---

46) Lindblom, op.cit. pp.3-17.
47) Pizzorno, op.cit. pp. 247-284.
48) Lowi, op.cit. pp. 52-56.

policy. What we can infer from Lowi is that politicians are also responsible for the results of interest group liberalism, so long as they have let groups demand more. On this point Samuel Huntington provides a similar argument, arguing that democracy is an uncontrollable regime, and elites are responsible for the demand explosion and government overload in the 1960s.[49]

Pluralism had a merit of describing the entity of groups in politics. It has been a reference model of a political system. What is missing or weak in its theory building is its treatment of the state. While the state is treated as arena where interest groups compete in pluralism, the state can exercise more power and influence than pluralists have thought it would do. With this necessity, scholars reopened their eyes for the "return of the State".

---

49) Samuel P. Huntington, "Democratic Distemper." *Public Interest*, no. 41. Fall 1975. pp.9-38.

4) Statism: The Statist approach to public policy

One of the weaknesses in group theory was its treatment of the state in its theory building. The state is regarded as an arena, and in an extreme conceptualization, the state is an interest group. A consequence of this treatment is obvious. The group theory could not well explain policy outcomes that are contrary to interest groups' demands. Furthermore, in generalization, group theory could not capture cases in which societal forces, including interest groups, are not well developed and therefore state took greater role in policy making.

Furthermore, a point that the power of the societal forces is relative to that of the state has been ignored or regarded as too natural in the pluralist picture. To make more generalizable arguments, arguments in group theory should be compensated by the role of the state; i.e., where groups are weak, the state takes greater role, and the state is an actor that can form and encourage interest group formation. This point brings us a motivation to turn to "Statism".

In this section, I will begin with a background story that brought a new emphasis on the "state", in the name of the return of the state. Then, I will review core elements of the theory. Thirdly, implication we can extract from the state-society relations will be discussed focusing representation issues.

4.1. Backgrounds for the return of the State

In Political Science, the concept of the state has been a major research topic. During the turn of the 19th century into early 20th century, a major paradigm shift occurred from the old institutionalism to the realism. In this, Political Science yielded invaluable master pieces still cited today, including writings by Vilfredo Pareto, Max Weber, Emile Durkheim, Woodrow Wilson, and Robert Michels. What realism brought in was "unbundling and disaggregating" of the abstract concepts including the "state".[50]

Some time later, the second wave of disaggregation of the state concept landed in Political Science. In classical pluralism, for example by Harold Laski, State is described as an association. Further elaboration in Pluralism, by Charles E. Lindblom's incremental decision making, argued that the virtue of decentralized bargaining over decisions by the centralized government.[51]

Still influenced by the realist trend, the third wave of unbundling came with Structural-Functionalism by Talcott Parsons and Systems theory by David Easton.[52] In these models, state and other social institutions were decomposed from their abstract entities and described in biological metaphors. By importing biological metaphors, functionalism and its adjacent systems theory again reduced the state into a model. State contents are claimed to be evaporated out of the model by critics.

Against this trend of theory development, there arose

---

50) Gabriel Almond, "The Return to the State," *American Political Science Review.* vol 82. no.3. September 1988. p.869.
51) Charles E. Lindblom, *The Intelligence of Democracy:* The Decision Making through Mutual Adjustment pp.102-116.
52) Talcott Parsons, *Politics and Social Structure* The Free Press. New York. 1969. pp.8-33.

a reversal of the trend, which is now called the "return of the state", by the adoption of a relatively loose concepts of the state and society.

4.2. Core elements in Statist Approach

(Bureaucracy)

One of the fore runners in the trend to bring the state back in was Theda Skocpol. In her work(1979), she conceptualized that the state, as a macro structure, is a set of administrative, policing, and military organizations headed and coordinated by executive authority.[53] As shown in Skocpol's case, in theorizing, statists can be characterized as utilizing the concept of bureaucracy. Bureaucracy is an embodiment of the state, and observable unit of analysis which allows researchers to utilize it as a tool for a middle range theory for their comparative purposes. This tradition of research

---

53) Theda Skocpol, *State and Social Revolution:* A Comparative Analysis of France, Russia, and China. Cambridge University Press. 1979. p.29.

can be rooted back to Max Weber, and therefore statist approach utilizing bureaucracy is called Weberian tradition. In Weberian tradition, researchers also studied value orientations of bureaucrats, to say nothing of the structure.   Another   tradition   is   more   a   macro perspective incorporated into statist argument, named as Tocquevillian   tradition.[54]   In   my   view,   these   two perspectives   are   not   necessarily   mutually   exclusive; Skocpol, for example, combines both.

Through Max Weber's social science, there is a common thread that pierce through his entire research. Weber explains the development as the "dymystification of the world, i.e. freeing the world from the spells of magic. In turn, this meant secularization of the world. People could pursue formal rationality, the essence of which was calculability. Formal rationality provided people with predictability and calculability. With this trend of rationalization, bureaucracy was the form of organization that corresponds to the demands of rationalization. Bureaucracy itself is an embodiment of

---

54) Theda Skcopol et al. ed., *Brining the State back in.* Cambridge Cambridge University Press. 1985. p.21.

rationalization that pursue efficiency, Also Weber's notion of bureaucracy is based on legal rational type of authority that is impersonal and predictable. With this foundation, bureaucracy promised the efficiency of administration.

(Main Arguments)
Bureaucracy as a key component of State Building

With this machine-like bureaucracy, Statists' claims were formulated in following ways. First, bureaucracy is considered as the core for the state-building. In Hans Rosenberg's analysis, Prussian bureaucracy was formulated through a dynamic process of state buildin g.[55] The Prussian Kings, in their efforts to build an autocracy, needed to check nobility class. To do so, they strengthened a new career bureaucracy equipped with technical competence and loyalty to their Dynasty. Although there has been a partial reversal of this development of a modern bureaucracy based on

---

55) Hans Rosenberg, *Bureaucracy, Aristocracy, and Autocracy:* The Prussian Experience 1660-1815. Cambridge, Massachusetts. Harvard University Press. 1958.

technical competence, due from fear of a Frederick William II that his bureaucracy would take control of power, an overall trend was cemented to consolidate the new bureaucracy as a vital component of state buildin g.[56] In Skocpol's analysis of Revolution, whenever there is a revolution, revolutionaries put their emphasis to either take control of the existing bureaucracy or to create a new bureaucracy to carry out their policies.

The Autonomy of the State

The second line of argument by statists is on the notion of state autonomy. A State is an autonomous actor. The autonomy is not a fixed structural feature of any governmental system.[57] Rather the concept implies that the nature of state action that is independent of social, economic, and personal ties.[58] In other words, state autonomy shows the state that is not captured by societal forces, like in pluralism.[59]

---

56) Rosenberg, op.cit. pp.202-228.
57) Skcopol, et al. *Bringing the State back in.* op.cit. p.14.
58) Skocpol, op.cit. p.10.
59) Also this notion of the state differs from a Marxist variant, instrumental Marxism, in which the state is just an instrument of the capitalist class.

A peculiar aspect is that scholars have been focusing on autonomous character of bureaucrats when they try to capture the image of autonomous state. Thus, in this line of theorizing, researchers had to emphasize conditions that would produce characteristics of bureaucrats that present state autonomy. Trimberger added to Stephan's arguments on the values and ideologies of bureaucrats. Trimberger argues, " a bureaucratic apparatus can be regarded as autonomous when bureaucrats are not recruited from the dominant industrial, landed, and commercial interest classes and when these bureaucrats do not have personal ties with the interests.[60]

International circumstances

Thirdly, statists have emphasized the importance of international circumstances that contribute to the formation and development of the state autonomy. Skocpol's major examples show how state became autonomous against the urgent international pressures in

---

60) Skocpol, op.cit. p.10.

the Russian case. Similarly, Trimberger emphasizes the foreign impact on the national autonomy. Foreign impact works as a trigger to the revolution from the above.

Strong state vs. Weak state

One of the statist arguments was developed into a strong state and weak state dichotomy.[61] By utilizing this framework, researchers could escape the problems associated with defining the state.

In sum, statism contributed to theory building for public policy in that it challenged and undermined the most encompassing, deterministic assumptions in pluralism, structural-functionalism, which is linked to development theories, and different versions of Marxism in which state lacks autonomy.

---

61) Peter Katzenstein, *Between Power and Plenty*, The University of Wisconsin Press. 1978. p.324.

4.3. Critical Analysis

State-Society issue I: representation in public policy

The theory of state emphasizes the capacity of the state in formulating, and implementing policies. The embodiment of the state, bureaucracy, is a representation of an efficient administration. Against this aspect of public policy, a remaining question is on the representative nature of bureaucracy: i.e. is public policy making through bureaucracy represents interests of the people? To be more theoretical, it is a question on the relationship between bureaucracy and democracy.

From Weber's notion of bureaucracy, bureaucracy's merit comes from its efficiency and neutral competence its incumbents have. In a critical thinking, it is reasonable to argue that bureaucracy's claimed virtue of efficiency and competence that results technical competence do not guarantee democratic representativeness.

Through the U.S history, as Herbert Kaufman points out, the focal point on administration has been shifted among three core values imposed on bureaucracy. Representation was emphasized during the early period of the U.S. history. Then, it turned out that "spoils system" and other electoral system do not produce healthy representation.[62]

Growing complexity of social problems requested more competence of bureaucracy and administration. As a result, fragmentation of bureaucracies occurred. These agencies were turned out to be captives of interest groups.[63] It is questionable whether the capture means representation of the people in policy making. If not, reliance on the state for public policy inevitably reduces representation of the people.

Despite this aspect, there are two ways to cure the problem. One is to strengthen administrative leadership vis- a-vis career bureaucracy. On this point Kaufman and Lowi agrees greatly, while there exists a difference on how to actually implement and exercise strong

---

62) Herbert Kaufman, "Emerging Conflicts in the Doctrines of Public Administration," *American Political Science Review,* vol 50. no 4. Summer 1956. p.1055.
63) Kaufman, op.cit. p.1062.
Lowi, op. cit. pp. 57-59.

administrative leadership.[64] The other solution is to resort to post modernistic, communitarian ideas, which will be discussed toward the end of this chapter.

State-Society issue II: Consequences of the state dominance

Another issue related to representation is on the consequences of state dominated interest representation. On this issue, at least two possibilities can be presented. One is a possibility for authoritarianism, and the other is that of corporatism. Under authoritarianism, usually, scholars discuss ruling coalition which is composed of bureaucrats, local businessmen, and other interest representation. In corporatism researches, government and interest representing "peak associations" exchange legitimacy for representing interests. In some sense, Corporatism can be understood as a way to overcome the "government overload" phenomenon which was common in western societies.[65] One interesting

---

64) Kaufman op.cit. pp.1062-1063.

point, in my view, is a consequence of studying the state dominated interest representation. It seems inevitable for scholars studying on interest representation from state-led perspective to reintroduce societal forces again in the theoretical scene. It is where historical institutionalism emerges. The historical institutionalism shares with statist approach in that both approaches tend to incorporate historical analysis, while historical institutionalism has wider scope for research.

5) Historical Institutionalism

Historical institutionalism shares its root with statist approach in several ways. One is that both approaches tend to utilize historical explanations. Second, both shares their discontent on the similar existing theories

---

65) Michel Crozier and Samuel Huntington, *The Crisis of Democracy* Report on the Governability of Democracies to the Trilateral Commission., New York, New York University Press. 1975.

prior to theirs. If I extend on the second point, following argument can be made for the background for the advent of historical institutionalism.

As was the case for the advent of statism, old institutionalism was impotent in developing intermediate level framework for comparative researches.[66] A response to this came in the form of behavioralism which focused on informal distribution of power, attitudes and political behavior. Behavioralists tried to overcome the ineffective explanation utilizing formal structures and reified structures in Marxist analysis. Behavioralists, however, could not explain cross-national differences of political behavior, and secondly, grand theorizing obscured different roles of the intermediating institutions that structure politics in different countries. With this backdrop, historical institutionalists came in the scene to offer an explanation for cross-national divergence through institutions.

---

66) Sven Steinmo et al. ed., *Structuring Politics*: Historical Institutionalism in Comparative Analysis Cambridge University Press 1992. p.3

5.1. State-Society issue: Representation in historical institutionalism

The most conspicuous aspect of the historical institutionalism is that interest representation is carried out by diverse institutions; in addition, institutions do shape preferences of the society. Thus, in this part, by reviewing the core arguments of the approach, I will discuss the issue of representation in historical institutionalism.

First, institutionalists argue that institutions constrain and refract politics, but they are not the sole cause of outcomes; institutions structure the process and by doing so influence outcomes. Thus, a main-question by historical institutionalists is how socio-economic, historical, organizational, and political processes shape interests. It is comparable to pluralist picture, in which theory mostly tells about representation from interest groups to a polity, rather than directly shaping interests. In conducting researches to study the main question, historical institutionalism offers fluidity and flexibility in accommodating diverse national, historical experiences.

Second, in relation to the first point, in historical institutionalism, the state is not a sole, dominant actor. Thus, a wider web of institutions, together with the state, determines the final outcomes, while the state still has a significant part in shaping the content and definition of interests through i) the contents and consequences of policy measures, ii) the incentives that particular regime types can provide, and iii) the authoritarian distribution of public status to interest groups.

In Peter Gourvetich's *Politics in Hard Times*, he compares policy responses of different countries during the three crises periods. Gourvitch laid out five policy options and five major social science explanations for a macro social phenomenon of policy coalition change.[67] Through his analysis, one can find dynamic fluidity in

---

67) Peter Gourevitch, *Politics in Hard Times*: Comparative Responses to International Economic Crises. Ithaca and London, Cornell University Press.
Kathleen Thelen., "Regulating Uber: The Politics of the Platform Economy in Europe and the United States" 23 November 2018 Perspectives on Politics. Volume 16 Issue 4 (Published online by Cambridge University Press)

each nation's case, how historical pattern, production profile, intermediate associations, and the state interact to produce different results. Through this way of conducting researches, a researcher can not be a captive of either society-centered theory like pluralism or state-centered view where the state takes the lion's share in explaining the outcomes. Instead, there is much room to incorporate different institutions in the political arena. For example, as intermediate associations filled the societies after the first crisis, in the second crisis these institutions took their share in shaping the political landscape; a typical institutionalist argument presents that these institutionalists shaped the preferences of their members.

Third, the notions on the common functions of interest groups are changed in the historical institutionalism. The traditional roles of interest groups, such as transmission and articulation of societal demands into political process, have largely disappeared. The new roles are socializing its citizens, organizing consensus, and making policies. Thus, in institutionalism, there is no longer the division of labor among political parties, interest groups and government. The form of interest representation in various countries is reformulated as different divisions of labor among these institutions occur.

5.2. Advantages and disadvantages of the historical institutionalist approach

At least two advantages of the approach can be articulated as follows. First, historical institutionalism can capture policy continuity and policy variations in a framework that connects different variables. In other words, historical institutionalism aims at the middle range theory that confronts issues of historical contingency and path-dependency.

Second, there is another virtue of utilizing the middle range framework of institutions. By using it, institutionalists could have analytic bridges between state centered and society centered theories. Furthermore, through middle range tools, institutionalists could mediate the effects of macro level socioeconomic structure and provide greater analytic leverage to explain variations across countries.[68]   For example, in historical institutionalism, we can know under what conditions, class differences figure into how groups and individuals in different capitalist countries define their interests.

Despite this refined virtue of the approach, its vulnerable point comes exactly from its strong point. It is the lack of parsimony in the historical institutionalism. While it is necessary to have many variables to have a fine picture, it is disadvantageous in finding a causality. In a cynical way, in historical institutionalism, there are always at least more then are causes that can be attributed to the outcomes in the model, because so diverse variables are put together.

6) Rational Choice Institutionalism

While both historical institutionalism and rational

---

68)   Steinmo, op.cit. p.11.

choice institutionalism share a common ground that institutions shape political preferences and influence political outcomes, these two different schools differ on their notion on how preferences formulated. While in historical institutionalism preferences are indigenously formulated within the framework of institutions, in rational choice institutionalism, interests are exogenously given.[69] In rational choice institutionalism, a research focus is given on how individually rational, self-interested actors formulate collective outcomes under the influence of institutions which act as constraints; in this analysis, institutions are deeply related to incentive structures of the society. In theorizing, rational choice theorists. starting from a micro foundation, build up to explain historical, macro phenomenon with their framework. Despite a divergence between theories among rational choice theories, unchanging theoretical components are the understanding of human beings as rational maximizers, and incentive structures that

---

69) Steinmo, op.cit. pp.8-9.
    Stephen Quackenbush, "The Rationality of Rational Choice Theory", Empirical and Theoretical Research in International RelationsVolume 30, 2004 - Issue 2

influence the individuals[70].

A forerunner of this approach, Mancur Olson, in his logic of collective action, challenges the pluralist notion that any voice can be heard by showing conditions for group formation. Individually rational actors could not produce a collective good when there were not much incentives. Olson argues that any large interest group needs selective incentives other than collective goods for their existence and maintenance.

Olson showed his consistency in his theory building on rational choice approach. In his book (1982), The Rise and Fall of Nations, he develops his insights that starts from rational individuals and their collective action problem to historical analysis after world war II on why economic growth rates differ across countries, by continuing his criticism on pluralism.[71]Against the claimed virtue of pluralism, the book suggests that in advanced democratic societies, the number of specific

---

70) Elinor Ostrom, *Governing the Commons:* The Evolution of Institutions for Collective Action. Cambridge university press, 1990.
71) Mancur Olson, *The Rise and Fall of Nations:* Economic Growth, Stagflation, and Social Rigidities. Yale University Press New Haven and London. 1982. pp.36-73.

interests has been increased and these increased interests are the sources of problems. The longer a society has enjoyed associational freedom in its history, the more possibility that the interest groups can meet propitious conditions. Once this condition is met, interest groups would not be disintegrated.

In these stabilized societies, special interests formulated will be a barrier to technological changes and new entries into markets. These series of actions would decrease efficiency and dynamics of the economy, and those interests would tend to be stronger and eventually hamper the speed of development of the society. On the other hand, Olson argues, societies where these interest groups have been destroyed by wars or revolutions, showed brilliant achievements in economic performance.

Douglas North, also in rational choice institutionalism tradition, presents his understanding of history, especially history on institutional change and economic performance. In presenting his thesis, his peculiar contribution comes from the term "path dependency". The term is utilized to show once incentive structure is set, how it reinforces individuals to produce divergent outcomes. Thus, in comparing Spain and England in 16th and 17th century, North shows how institutional disincentives have "badly" influenced in Spain to reduce economic vitality.[72]

7) The Communitarian Approach

The communitarian approach brings us an opportunity to criticize pluralism, and support the classical participatory democratic theory. Thus, communitarian approach is revisiting the classical debate on participation from a bottom-up building of a theory.

7.1. In support of the feasibility of Participatory democracy

In the classical democratic theory, there has been a debate on the feasibility of participation. In Rousseau's view, participation is virtuous thing, and becoming possible through education of people. Against this view

---

72) Douglas North, *Institutions, Institutional Change, and Economic Performance*, Cambridge University Press. 1990. pp.114-115

are arguments that present dismal pictures on the feasibility of participatory democracy. These arguments include an argument that low socio-economic status group people tend to lack qualification for participatory democracy.

While more and more researches have been accumulated in support of the dismal and infeasible nature of participatory democracy, the room for participation was filled with representation. The typical embodiment of the representation, utilizing interest groups as vehicles of representation, was pluralism. In pluralism, it was strongly assumed that a system of interest group representation is a realistic approximation of what a modern democracy can be in a world that is more complex than Rousseau's world.

Pluralism, however, has been under attack by diverse viewpoints. One of the possibility that un-participatory nature of interest groups may develop. The second criticism is what Lowi and Etzioni agree on the special interest groups' capture of the government. The third is participatory democracy's tendency to fall into an unrestrained uprising of demands.[73]

7.2 Suggestions by Communitarians

The cure for these three symptoms of pluralism comes from a community-based approach in communitarianism. Communitarian authors agree on a point that solutions come from ways of strengthening communities. Etzioni, in this context, articulates his agenda as follows; Communitarian ideal materialized by Etzioni is not to abandon the legacy of the modern era in pursuing a post modern communitarian platform. Rather, what he has suggested is how to harmonize and maintain balance between diversity (the virtue of pluralism) and unity (the virtue of communitarianism). To rephrase it, Etzioni proposes that it is necessary to strengthen communitarian elements in the urban and suburban centers to provide social bonds.

What communitarians are claiming is to start at the local level where interests of residents are directly and easily expressed. Berry brings in an argument that

---

73) Samual P. Huntington, "The Democratic Distemper," Public Interest, no. 41. Fall 1975. pp.9-38.

where these community based interests are formed, these interests defend community interests against that of business.[74]Etzioni's platform is wider in scope in articulating and including moral values as well as plans to create social bonds (glues) to rebuild community. Etzioni includes in his platform[75] ideas of i) restoring moral values, ii) a new role of government, and iii) a new way to prevent corruption in politics.

(Assessment)

After reviewing communitarian ideas, it is inevitable to assess its appeals and weakness. On its weakness, following remarks can be presented. Since classical democratic theory on, it has been a recurring question whether "participatory" democracy can overcome the problem of "scale". Berry is also presenting a balanced view on the feasibility of community based participatory democracy. In this sense, it may be reasonable to argue that communitarian approach has not completely

---

74) Jeffrey M. Berry et al., The Rebirth of Urban Democracy, The Brookings Institution, Washington, D.C. 1993.
75) Amitain Etzinoi, *The Spirit of Community* : Rights, and The Communitarian Agenda. Crown Publishers, Inc. New York. 1993. pp.251-267.

overcome the problem.

With a slightly different angle, however, this is not a serious drawback of the approach. Following Etzioni's line of logic, communitarian ideal is to be complemented with the legacy of the past and present industrial society contexts; thus, it is possible say that the focus of feasibility discussion should not be on the scale issue, but on the practical feasibility in the urban, and suburban settings. Whether it is practically possible to restore social bonds to produce the desired outcomes would be a key question on the feasibility.

Then, what are the appeals of this approach? On this, in my view, three points can be presented. First, as we agree, the development of capitalism destroyed social values by commodifying labor and breaking social glues that held societies in unity. Communitarian approach is appealing because it is emphasizing the restoration of the glues without sacrificing rationalized living styles of a modern man. Second, for policy makers, it is a new influx of ideas to resolve current dilemmas. Today, to improve policy outcomes, there are two ways of doing it; one is reinventing government, and the other is inducing communities to participate and therby increase effectiveness. This appeal would be greater at the local level. Third, also for scholars, communitarianism offers a fresh challenge against what we have built up on the rationalization of the world.

A Concluding Remark of the Theoretical Framework

Through this paper, I have reviewed different theories on their core contents and state-society issues. Upon concluding the paper, I would like to present several points on how to utilize these different theories in the study of public policy.

First, it is reasonable to state that the relevance of each theory depends on the nature of policy areas. Second, fitness of a theory to a context also depends on a factor whether the purpose of a research is a prescriptive or an academic one. Third, another point to mention is a wise use of both political science developed theories and other social science theories in the analysis of public policy. For example, decision making theories are not necessarily in conflict with bureaucracy theory. Similarly, implementation studies can be utilized in connection with other theories I discussed in this book.

Social science theories are like software of a society. Thus, depending on a wise use of it, the efficacy of public policy would be enhanced exponentially. The responsibility of not only developing, but also well utilizing appropriate theories is on the scholars in public policy.

2. Theory of Bureaucracy and Its Impacts on the Public Sector and Public Policy

1) Prologue

Max Weber's Bureaucracy has been a baseline in understanding modern organizations. In the public sector, bureaucracy has been a pivotal element of administration and implementation of policies. Weber, based on his notion of development of rationality in the world, claims that bureaucracy is the embodiment of the formal rationality and is the most efficient organizational form. Since Weber, a lot of different streams of criticisms and amendments were suggested on his ideal type bureaucracy. This part will discuss what are the main line of criticisms on bureaucracy, then also discuss whether current development in the public sector offers a new angle to consider bureaucratic organizations.

Two baselines can be presented at this moment. One baseline argument in this essay is that despite numerous criticisms, Weber's ideal type bureaucracy is still a valuable reference frame and those criticisms helped to elaborate actual working conditions and dynamics of bureaucracy in the real world. Weber himself was the most concerned person on the consequences that rationalization of the world (for example iron cage of capitalism) and bureaucracy as an embodiment of rationalization would bring. The ideal type Bureaucracy presented by Weber, however, has a value as a theoretical construct which serves as a platform for theory development. Furthermore, no wonder weber knew that bureaucratic model would entail dysfunctional aspects as well. The second one is how to understand the current development of the public sector. In this essay, I attempted to define current developments as a trend towards cutback management and increasing efficiency in the government which I think is a recurring theme in the history of organizational theory. The last part will briefly mention on the contribution of organization theory to public policy studies.

2) Characteristics of Bureaucracy in Max Weber and its Technical Superiority

2.1 Characteristics

For Weber, bureaucracy was a consequence of rationalization which freed the world from the spells of magic. Bureaucracy was an organizational machine based on legal, rational authority. According to Weber, a fully developed bureaucracy is the most efficient organizational form. In this section, I will present characteristics of Weber's ideal type bureaucracy.

First, a bureaucracy is a continuous organization of official functions bounded by rules and organized in a clearly defined hierarchy of offices; through this hierarchical order, authority and command is exercised.

Second, an ideal type bureaucracy features impersonality. Incumbents of the offices in a bureaucracy are subject to authority of the superiors only with respect to their impersonal official obligations. For these incumbents, a strict division of the public and the private spheres is found. This feature distinguishes modern bureaucracy based on rational/ legal authority with patrimonial bureaucracy.

Third, recruitment: The basis of recruitment of incumbents is their technical competence(expertise) to the tasks. Usually expertise is proved through tests or certificates.

Fourth, career: Incumbents consider their positions in the offices as career jobs or primary occupation. This means a bureaucracy as a career system with promotion system.

Fifth, bureaucrats are remunerated by fixed salaries in money. This shows a distinction of the private and the public spheres, and a separation of incumbents' position from the ownership of the means of administration.

Sixth, bureaucracy can be represented by its formalism and documentation practices. So administrative acts, decisions, and rules are formulated and recorded in writings(documents). This guarantees the continuity of the administration.

2.2 Sources of Technical Superiority

The primary source of the superiority of bureaucratic organization lies in the role of technical knowledge. Then, what are the components of this technical knowledge? First, it is the continuity of tasks. Second, it is the predictability of actions bureaucracy would take. This is attained through documentation, formalism, and impersonalism which ideal type bureaucracy features.

3) Amendments of Weber's ideal type Bureaucracy

In this section, I will discuss how original ideal type bureaucracy model has been criticized, amended, and thereby became closer to the working conditions of the real world. I will divide the discussion into following manner. First, I will discuss issues on the internal structure of bureaucracy and individuals within the structure. These issues encompass structural dysfunctions of bureaucratic organizations, cultural aspects of bureaucracy that resist change, and the relationship between organizations and individuals. Second, I will discuss the issues of decision making in organizations, examining whether bureaucratic form organizations are efficient organizations, because of Weber's original scents. Third, I will explore the relationship between bureaucracy and its environments. This part will be devoted to two things. One is bureaucracy and democracy issue; the other is organizations' struggle for survival.

3.1. Ammendment 1: issues on the bureaucratic structure and individuals within the structure

Dysfunctional Aspects of the Structure

Robert Merton questioned the concept of rational bureaucracy in his "bureaucratic structure and personality". His central topic was the displacement of goals, due to over-comformity to rules.[76] He begins with the necessity for control from the top level of organization. Subordinates are asked to stick to SOP (standard operating procedures), and controls are carried out whether a personell abode by the procedures. A consequence of this over-conformity to rules is the displacement goals; rules that were originally created to attain goals now have their own meaning, and individuals in bureaucratic organizations would become rigid in their behaviors. Merton expressed this as "trained incapacities"; a person, who would be able unless he was trained, became incapacitated after being trained in a bureaucratic form of organization.

---

76) Robert Merton, Ailsa P.Gray, Barbara Hockey, Hanan C.Selvin, Reader in Bureaucracy, 1952. pp.361-371

One consequence from this phenomenon is bureaucracy's possible reaction to citizens. Bureaucracy would try to defend itself against demands for reform, and would conflict with citizens.[77]

Philip Selznick, also starting from the necessity, presents on the delegation of authority and its consequences. He argues that delegation of authority contributes to the attainment of goals, and then delegation is expanded. This, however, would bring "parochialism" between sub-units, because the delegation requires specialization which would be accompanied with high education costs of members, and thereby each sub-unit's interests depend on zero-sum nature games.

Victor Thompson introduces "personal insecurity" in his description of "bureau-pathology".[78] He argues that bureaucracy tends to foster specific responses of bureaucrats including resistence to change.

As an extension of Merton and Selznick, Alvin Gouldner mentioned on how control technology that

77) Martin Albrow, Bureaucracy1970, Pall Mall Press, pp.54-55
78) Thompson, Victor A. *Modern organization.* University of Alabama Press, 1977.

aimed at maintaining equilibrium of subunits destroy entire system, and how it is feed backed to sub systems.[79] Rules that suggest minimum level of performance standards would lead individuals to have minimal level of knowledge of acceptable performance and real performance according to that level. Superiors, knowing this, would increase direct controls, and thereby increases tensions. To reduce this tension, more impersonal rules have to be applied. Gouldner, in his example of mining company, pointed out following things. He argued that Weber only focused on making structure, and neglected the process on who are making rules, to whom the rules offer legitimacy, whose values will be encroached when rules are applied and, how rules affect the status of members in an organization.

Peter Blau also contributed on the relationship between rules and rational administration. Blau studied a United States federal law enforcement agency and a state employment agency. In employment agency, the

---

79) Alvin Gouldner, Patterns of Industrial Bureaucracy, Free Press, Glencoe, IL, 1954.
Martin Albrow, op.cit., pp.56-57

central procedures for finding jobs for the unemployed are modified so that each official's performance in allocating jobs was statistically recorded. Blau found that a group of officials who cooperate with each other and pay little attention to statistical assessments were more productive than those who are stimulated to be competitive by the records. Blau's contribution comes from the point that he suggested a new criteria for rational administration; he argued," in a changing environment, the stable attainment of organizational objectives depends on perpetual change in the bureaucratic structure. Therefore, efficiency cannot be guaranteed by tethering the official to a set of rigid rules." He also continued that efficient administration can be attained only when a bureaucrat is allowed to identify with the purposes of the organization as a whole and to adapt his behavior to hie perception of changing circumstances.[80]

---

80) Martin Albrow, op.cit., p.58

The relationship between individuals and organization

The second issue under the internal structure is the relationship between individuals and organization. Although this topic overlaps with the preceding section in some sense, in this section, I will present Chris Argyris's argument.[81] He claims that human beings have desires for self-actualization through the completion of mature personality, despite the difference in place, timing, and intensity. He claimed that this desire is completely constrained by the modern bureaucratic organizations. According to him, modern bureaucratic organizations request following things to individuals. They ask individuals minimal control on their routinized tasks, expect them to be passive, dependent, submissive to organizations. Bureaucracy expects individuals to have "short term "perspective, and want them to master only small number of superficial knowledge with perfection by repetition, and induce them to place higher value on their jobs. Also bureaucracy leads them to a situation

---

81) Chris Argyris, Personality and Organization, New York Harper, 1957
Chris Argyris, Integrating the Individual and the Organization, New York. Routledge 2017

where individuals can experience "psychological failures". In other words, organizations request people to maintain infantile personality at least during work hours, and this conformity is linked to possibilities for wage increase and promotion. Alternatives for individuals are therefore, exit or loyalty. In some sense, I can suggest a possibility for alienation in the Argyris's picture.

2.1 Ammendment 2: issues on decision making

The second big stream of ammendment of Weber's Bureaucracy comes from the tradition of decision making in organizations. First, I will discuss Simon and March's contributions. Then, secondly, I will discuss "group think" argument and Bureaucratic politics. Finally, in this section, this section will present other ammendments to Weberian Bureaucracy related to decision making.

Bounded Rationality

Herbert Simon challenged the traditional notion of rational decision maker by introducing the concept of satisficing and bounded rationality. His example of selecting the sharpest niddle among a pile of niddles suggested man's limited capacity to compare between alternatives.[82] From the notion of bounded rationality, we can infer that decision makers compare alternatives in a restricted way. This is a point where Weberian bureaucracy in the real world is constrained by individual decision maker's ability as well as limitation of capacity of organization as a problem solver.

Group Think

In Irving Janis's victims of group think, I can present a possible disaster in the decision making process. The example was the decision to attack Cuban seashores. In the decision process, due to the group process that strengthened the conformity, correct information was buried, and the decision to attack was adopted.[83]

---

82) March, James G. "Bounded rationality, ambiguity, and the engineering of choice." The bell journal of economics (1978): 587-608.
March, James G. "Bounded rationality, ambiguity, and the engineering of choice." The bell journal of economics (1978): 587-608.

Information filtering, authority leakage, and error correction

Another important feature in bureaucratic organization with hierarchical structure is that information should be reduced to be reached from the bottom to the top level. This phenomenon, in some sense, seems natural. However, when middle level incumbents exercise their bias in filtering information, rationality of the decision will be undermined. On the other hand, there is a phenomenon called "authority leakage". When a top level decision maker initiates a decision, as the issue comes down the hierarchy, the intention, the issue, or the agenda can be amplified, or distorted; this also undermines the rationality of ideal type bureaucracy. But these phenomena offer more exact description of the organizational life.

---

83) Janis, Irving L. "Groupthink." IEEE Engineering Management Review 36.1 (2008): 36.
Janis, Irving L. Victims of Group Think 1973.
Janis, I. (1991). Groupthink. In E. Griffin (Ed.) A First Look at Communication Theory (pp. 235 - 246). New York: McGrawHill.

3.3. Ammendment 3: Bureaucracy and its environments

This section will discuss about the interaction between bureaucracy and its environments; first, this part will present arguments on the relationship between bureaucracy and democracy. Then, a focal point will be given to interaction between bureaucracy and its task environment.

Bureaucracy and Democracy

Weber himself was concerned about the consequences rationalization would bring. He expressed his anxiety on the consequences of the development of capitalism and bureaucracy that were results of rationalization. Even in Weber's notion of Bureaucracy, there is a contradiction on the character of bureaucracy; bureaucracy was described as a tool, and at the same time it was described as autonomous, due to its expertise and skill. Scholars after Weber pondered on this problem of bureaucracy and power. Reinhard Bendix argued that modern bureaucracy has monopoly of skill and monopoly of power.[84] Monopoly of skill makes administrative personnel highly irreplacable, and monopoly of power even makes a revolution nearly impossible in advanced countries without having control of bureaucracy.[85]

This notion of bureaucracy's power is discussed in a way whether it can be a threat to democracy. The main focal point of discussion was what is the limitation of bureaucracy's power. Bendix argues that having skilled personnel in bureaucracy does not mean the monopoly of skill, and autonomy increases as the bureaucracy grows, but this does not mean the monopoly of power. Thus, it may be reasonable to state that bureaucracy's autonomy and power is pre-defined; this becomes clear when we see where does the power of bureaucracy derive? If the power and autonomy derives from sovereignty, then the limits of bureaucracy becomes evident.

---

84) Reinhard Bendix, Bureaucracy and the problem of power, in Robert merton ed. Reader in Bureaucracy, pp.114-118

85) Bendix, op.cit., p.118
Similar notion is found in Crane Brinton, The anatomy of revolution

Bureaucracy and its task environment: survival and uncertainty control

In original Weber's conception, Bureaucracy is a machine that carries out orders and rules. What is missing in Weber's picture is a consideration for interaction between bureaucracy and its environments. Scholars of bureaucracy and organizations showed that bureaucracy, if it intends to work as a machine, should be adapted to its environments; and this results in a dissolution of ideal type image. In the face of environments, organizations and bureaucracies tend to preserve themselves by pursuing its survival. Especially, literatures on Public bureaucracies have shown how bureaucracies have pursued its survival.

Selznick's concept of cooptation shows how a governmental agency acquire political legitimacy as well as local supporting grounds conducive for survival, by adopting new elements. Organizational studies on the issue of "goal displacement" can be understood in a similar context. Pressman and Wildavsky's implementation[86] can also be interpreted in a way to support Bureaucracy's staying power to overcome "joint decision problems" and survive to fulfil its duties.

Bureaucracy's endeavors to preservation and survival are well elaborated in the wors of James D. Thompson, Harvey Sapolsky, Wildavsky, and Parkinson's works.[87] James D. Thompson presents, in my view, two important concepts: technical core and boundary spanning.[88] James D. Thompson offers three sources of uncertainty for organizations, and argues that uncertainty control is the fundamental organizational problem and all complex organizations seek self-control or the ability to act independent of environmental forces. The three sources of uncertainty are, first, from the lack of clarity in cause & effect relationships in the society (external source), second, contingency or the uncertainty caused

---

86) Pressman, Jeffrey L., and Aaron Wildavsky. Implementation: How great expectations in Washington are dashed in Oakland; Or, why it's amazing that federal programs work at all, this being a saga of the Economic Development Administration as told by two sympathetic observers who seek to build morals on a foundation. Vol. 708. Univ of California Press, 1984.

87) Klimek, Peter, Rudolf Hanel, and Stefan Thurner. "Parkinson's Law quantified: three investigations on bureaucratic inefficiency." *Journal of Statistical Mechanics: Theory and Experiment* 2009.03 (2009): P03008.

88) Thompson, James D. *Organizations in action: Social science bases of administrative theory*. Routledge, 2017.
Thompson, James D. "Theory and Research in Administration." (1967): 691-694.

by the fact that the outcomes of organizational actions are determined by other organizations in the environments, and third, as an internal source independence of components or the uncertainty caused by the coordination requirements of the organization's technology (internal source).

Against these uncertainties, organizations tend to reduce uncertainty and try to protect their "technical core". An example of the term" technical core" can be found in Prof. Sapolsky's Polaris Missile development. The proponents of the missile development, after getting the budget approved, tried to maintain their intentions untacted from outside influences. They worried the outside scientists' influence that would change designs. At the same time, they needed legitimacy; thus, they coopted outside scientists, and used the PERT(program evaluation and review technique) to convince other interested people to protect the technical core(developing missile with their independence).

Another concept that is useful in explaining bureaucratic organization's survival efforts is "boundary spanning". The term was originally used to depict the role of "exeuctives" when they are expanding their connections to outside. In my view, public organizations also perform this function; maintaining good public relations is an example.

In addition to bureaucracy's efforts for survival, public bureaucracies are well known to be less responsive to environments. Public organizations not only try to survive, but they do not know how to curtail themselves. Parkinson's law presents bureaucracy's inclination to expand. Empirically in many countries, the size of bureaucracy expands cyclically until the time for political reform initiates the streamlining of the size of bureaucracy. Wildavsky's The politics of budgetary process is an example for survival and expansion. In the book, Wildavsky shows how bureaucrats behave in order to maintain their budgets in the subsequent years. One example is the behavior to use all the budgets allocated to an agency; because remaining portion would mean that the budgets will be curtailed in the subsequent fiscal years.

4) Whether we should view public sector from a different angle?

In the preceding section, I have discussed how Weber's Bureaucracy has been amended. In this section, based on what I have presented in the preceding section, I will discuss whether public bureaucracies in the current era can be viewed from a different angle.

March and Olson argue that administrative reform is an iterating phenomenon. From the administrative reform in the early 20th century in the U.S. on, each reform was aiming at introducing efficiency and effectiveness of bureaucracy.[89] March and Olson's understanding of the current reform is correct in that the reform movement is a recurring phenomenon. But there are some points, I can suggest as new considerations. First, I will elaborate today's situation, and then discuss the suggestions.

The time we are living at this current stage can be

---

89) March, James G. and Johan P. Olsen. Rediscovering Institutions: The Organizational Basis of Politics. Free Press. London and New York. 1995.

argued as the time when "steady, continuous economic growth cannot be guaranteed. Despite this fact, demands and rising expectations from societal forces are ever increasing. In addition, increasing complexity of social contexts have requested newer roles of government. For example, the advent of the intellectual rights as a property right would let government to legislate appropriate bills to protect them. In this situation, public bureaucracies are asked to respond to these tasks. The question is then, can bureaucracy take the burden, is it really capable of doing that?

As I have discussed in this essay with Parkinson's law, Bureaucracies tends to grow. Wilson and Clark argue that organizations try to persist, once they are created. Even in TVA case, this is true. The authority has been adapted to the "new" environment" in the sense that they have been constructing "nuclear power plants" that were not in their task lists at the time it was created.

Historically, since the world war II, bureaucracies in every country has been expanding. These bureaucracies were never curtailed, unless there were political reforms. Wildavsky's budgetary politics show a tendency of a bureaucracy to spend all their resources they are given in a fiscal year, lest they should lose or get reduced of their budget bases. Bureaucraices do resist changes in every country.

Under these backdrops, there are no new things for public bureaucracies. But with the same situation, there are something to remind us. First, it is not wise to burden government more with new demands. Although a researcher does not agree with neo-corporatist prescriptions, it is still meaningful to know that de-linking bureaucracies with burdens would increase its performance. Deregulation measures in Britain can be an example.

Second, national characteristics still matter in designing reforms. In March and Olson, I can find that due to the specific natures of the Scandinavian countries, they preferred administrative reform, instead of bold privatization.[90]

---

90) March and Olson, Rediscovering Institutions, pp.105-107

Third, in pursuing administrative reform, I think it is not always desirable to adopt private sector prescription directly into the public sector. In the article of Bo Rothstein, the Swedish government adopted "private sector prescription' by letting a consulting firm that consulted the SAS airline.[91] In my view the origin of failure was from the misunderstanding of the nature of public sector. Public sector has no output markets in which competition exists. Thus, privates sector prescription reduced street level bureaucrats' incentives to offer better services.

Briefly I have mentioned several suggestions on how to view public sector's reform of today. I argue that the basics of public bureaucracies have not changed. But there are necessities for changes. Thus, in exercising reform measures for increasing efficiency, it would be crucial not to forget the nature of the public sector.

---

91) Bo Rothstein, The crisis of the Swedish Social democrats and the future of the universal welfare state, Center for European Studies, March ,1992

Chapter 3

Contributions of institutional analysis for policy transfers and institutional re-design: Implications for Globalization of the Public Sector

Prologue

With increasing trend of globalization in every sphere of life, it is nearly impossible for us to think in an isolated way as past generations had done. Started mainly from private economic areas, globalization has started penetrating into areas where traditionally national and regional peculiarities were respected and therefore no such thing as global standards can be discussed. These areas include cultural spheres and more sensitively the areas of the public sector in which traditional concept based on sovereignty seems impossible to co-exist with the globalization and global standards themselves.

Despite the past trends and traditions, it is not unnatural these days to discuss the globalization of the public sector. This chapter, noting the change of environments, discusses the current status and achievements towards globalization in the Korean context and tries to illuminate clues to approach the seemingly mismatching phenomenon, i.e. the advanced institutional system and its lacking performance. A special focus is given to the analysis of civic culture and its foundations in Korea in analyzing the possible origin of the lacking development toward globalization in Korea. With the preceding discussion, this paper will carefully suggest future directions for improving public sector globalization in Korea.

1. Current Status and Achievements towards Globalization

1) An International Comparison

As interests on globalization being increased, international efforts to understand different degrees of globalization has taken place. Despite their validity still being questioned in terms of methodology including reliability of questionnaire and sampling frame, they still offer a good starting point to research globalization and its impact on diverse aspects of private and public sector.

Among diverse survey of its kind, one of the most well known report has been published by IMD. In this section, tis paper will review some of its data by processing it for the purpose of this chapter. The IMD report has, in fact, presented a variety of indicators to express global competitiveness. The list of indicators include overall competitiveness scores for each country, and specific sub-items for both government and the private sector. For example, the government related indicators include support for business, small government, market orientation, and budget related indicators, while overall scores of government in international comparison are well known to general public.

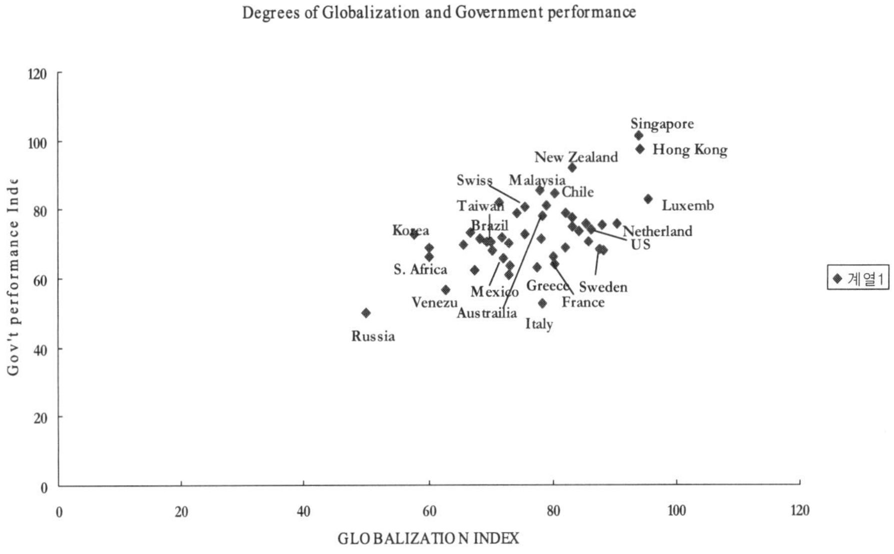

Degrees of Globalization and Government performance

Figure 1 Globalization and Gov't Performance

Figure 1 shows the plotting of globalization index

and government performance index for 46 countries. The data is based on 1996 IMD report, and this paper re-processed to present an overview that there exists a relationship between globalization and government performance index. From the figure, it is reasonable to argue that in general, so called advanced nations feature higher marks on globalization and government indexes. This suggest a possibility that there "is" or possibly "may be" a tendency or trend regarding the globalization of the government sector, assuming that advanced countries still have something that developing countries should learn.

2) Domestic Efforts to improve the Public Sector as harbingers towards Globalization

In the preceding section this chapter presented a status report by utilizing existing report on globalization. What was evident from the "picture" was that there is a direction toward which government sector can be improved, although actual dimensions of improvement for each country should be addressed in detailed efforts.

The impression from the IMD report has been that countries like Korea was not an impressive performer in overall indicators. Especially the government sector was marked lower than its private sector counterpart. While the report has been cited widely in Korea, questions regarding the validity of the evaluation method has always followed the citations. This offers a counter-intuitive question regarding what has been done in the improvement of public sector in Korea. In this section, this chapter will review the efforts undertaken by the Korean government so far to improve government in international standards.

Earlier Efforts

Scholars broadly agree that the discipline of public administration and its application influenced by the U.S. was first introduced in Korea during the early 1960s. It was the hay day for comparative politics focusing on developing countries, and this trend was imported in

Korea in the name of comparative public administration and development administration. While assumptions lied in these theories are controversial in today's standards, it is reasonable to argue that these became the harbingers of modernizing the public sector in global standards per se in the Korean society. Since its introduction, the discipline of public administration and its application has continuously influenced the public sector in Korea.

Improvements in Service Provision

While efforts to improve the government in the 1960s and 1970s were concentrated in enhancing efficiency in the government, a trend that has been visualized since the 1980s on was the emphasis on improving service provision, which is still being carried out in different policies. The importance of improving service provision in the government is that it is the most frequent contact point by citizens vis-à-vis the government, where the government's efficacy is being contested.[92]

Knowing this, the directions for improving service provision in Korea has started from reducing the waiting cues in the 'regional' field office, reducing difficulties in issuing public documents, including passport, and reforming government regulations closely affecting ordinary people's lives. These efforts were greatly enhanced with the introduction of information technology in the public offices.

2. Origins of dissatisfaction regarding the globalization of the Public Sector

1) Discrepancy

In the preceding section, this chapter has reviewed the current status of globalization efforts by the Korean government and survey results by an international

---

92) Lipsky, M., Street Level Bureaucracy: Street-Level Bureaucracy, 30th Anniversary Edition: Dilemmas of the individual in Public Services Russel Sage Foundation. New York 2010.

institution. From the juxtaposition of the two trends, i.e. reform efforts to enhance the level of public administration and lagging performance surveyed by the international organization present a cleft to be analyzed. The cleft can be described in two dimensions. While the first gap is the gap of perception in understanding the level of Public Administration between the Korean government and international institution, the second gap is the difference between the level of social capital and the development of public management in Korea.

This chapter argues that these gaps provide clues on why three parties, international organization, the Korean government, and general citizens in Korea, are all dissatisfied with their perception of globalization in the public sector. As shown in the figure, as for the Korean government, with its continuing reform activities from the past, it may think that the level of public administration has been greatly enhanced, while international institutions, such as IMD, has been presenting survey results quite opposite to the Korean government's expectation.

From the perspective of this chapter, a clue in understanding this discrepancy comes from the notion of "social capital" endowed in the Korean context. As a consequence of the inheritance of the existing "social capital" in the Korean context, what we observe is the gap between relatively advanced public sector management and slowly changing social capital that dramatically undermines the efficacy people feel about public sector performance, while social capital level offers sufficient condition for the low perception.

2) Social Capital Concpetualization and Its application from "Making Democracy Work: Civic Traditions in Modern Italy"

In his book, Making Democracy Work: Civic Traditions in Modern Italy, the author Robert Putnam[93] "revives" the civic culture approach which was fully

---

93) Robert Putnam, Making Democracy Work: Civic Traditions in Modern Italy 2001 Princeton University Press.

developed in the 1960s in Political Science in the behavioralism era. Civic Culture has been a major explanatory variable in persuading audience on the outcomes of a political system. On this foundation, what Putnam added was to link this prior foundation with his concept of "social capital" which he brings in from historical roots. The concept of social capital is Putnam's major determinant that produces divergence of institutional performance across southern and northern regional governments.

In developing his argument that areas with "rich" social capital, i.e. areas that have conducive environments for democracy and effective government, Putnam relied on several methodologies. First, in data gathering stage, he utilized panel data by asking the same group of people in his survey. Also he prepared various basic indicators which can be used as variables in his later analysis to produce composite indices. Second, in the analysis, he resorted to factor analysis as the statistical method.

For example, one of his examples of composite

indicators, the institutional performance, was constructed by utilizing variables (basic indicators) such as reform legislation, day care centers, housing and urban development, legislative innovation, cabinet stability, industrial policy instruments, and local health unit spending. For all these variables, factor loadings were calculated, and for a region's performance, these variables or basic indicators were added after by being factor loadings are multiplied to each variable.

After finishing this job of making a composite index of institutional performance, Putnam relies on "correlation" figures with other variables of interest; one example is correlation between civic community and institutional performance. With these correlation figures, he contrasted the difference between the south and the north. His analysis mainly stops at this stage, and in chapter 5, he traces a possible causal diagram.

(Critique)

Despite the fact that this book is written with elaboration, still there is room for criticism. First, by resorting to historical roots back into medieval periods, the author is making deterministic conclusion.

Second, in a narrow time frame, Putnam also presents that civic involvement in the 1900s had strong impacts on both civic involvement in the 1970s and economic development in the 1970s; with these two variables of the 1970s, he derives institutional performance of the 1980s in Italy. I suspect a missing link here. Although Putnam did not put an arrow between socio economic development in the 1970s and civic involvement in the 1970s, there must be a strong impact from the socioeconomic development to civic involvement. Thus, this chapter argue that Putnam mis-specified his model.

Then, how can this be convincing will be my next point, which I will briefly touch on. What I think is more convincing is a maturation along the industrialization. Above all, as industrialization takes place in the north, people moved from the South to the North following their opportunities; these people must have been most able-bodied people in the south and the likelihood of having "modern" civic value would be very high. A consequence is the even more depletion of civic social capital in the South. With a similar logic, if industrialization had taken place in the South, civic roots may have changed. Thus, if we can find immigration records from south to north from the 1900s on, we can approach a more convincing testbed for the "civic roots" argument.

Third, the fact that Putnam too much relies on correlation figures for his persuasion may be his weakness. Correlation can be just necessary conditions for causality.

His study tried to overcome the limitations of case study method by increasing implications from various regions in Italy; but in addition to this, in my view, if he could add cases from other countries on the relationship between civicness and democracy (institutional performance), we can see whether the civic roots argument would have persuasive power.

3) Difficiencies in Social Capital

Continuing from the argument that the notion of social capital provides clues for approaching the issue of global standrads in Public Administration, this chapter relies on a six country comparative survey on citizens' attitudes on 17 elements that can be regarded as components of social capital per se. Before elaborating selected components that are closely reflecting the status that social capital in Korea vis-à-vis other countries, it is possible to present a summary table on what elements Korean people featured functioning aspects of "social capital" and what dimensions they showed dysfunctioning elements.

Conducive Factors for Social Capital	Negative Factors for Social Capital
Attitudes toward collectivity: toward "Nation" → Reflecting the Nation-State charateristic	Attitudes toward collectivity: Low Citizenship → Less cultivated citizenship
	Negative attitudes for individual level participation for community service
Strong curiosity for Neighbors' activities	Relatively significant distance among neighbors → Early Modernization level
	Strong Insistence on one's will
Consciousness for conserving goods	Low preference for used products
	Relatively Low job satisfaction

Table 1 Factors of Social Capital

Attitudes on Collectivity

In general, one would think that Korean people are collectively oriented. With this perception, it is interesting to review the results from the survey. From the survey, indeed, Korean people marked the highest scores in overall scores for collectivistic attitudes. A closer look, however, reveals a different picture. Koreans showed a spectrum of results on different questions in this category. On a survey item, "What is good for a nation is good for myself"? Koreans showed the highest mark among the people in six countries, while on a survey item," public duties are more important than private matters" and "people in my country prioritize national interests over private interests", Koreans marked 4th and 6th among the six countries. These mismatching results imply that while Korean are aware of the consequences of collective action as a functional and positive one, internalization of the value has not taken place.

This low attitudes on collectivity is indirectly presented by another survey list. In a question, the survey asked citizens of different countries which country has highest attitudes toward collectivity. Citizens of Italy, Germany, and U.K. responded Korea as the lowest marked country, while people in the U.S. and Japan marked Korea as the 5th and 4th respectively. Korean people has their own self assessment by marking themselves as 4th among the six countries. What can be implied is that from the Western perspective where collectivism lies on civil society formation(Cohen), Korean society is regarded as lacking civicness per se.

Social Gathering with Neighbors and Community Service

Survey revealed that Korean people have strong curiosity on neighbors' issues, but at the same time showed relative distance in actual events. Table shows that Koreans showed the highest rank for their response on the survey list "I will always participate in community activities. Despite the seemingly positive side of neighborhood relations depicted in the above table, yet an opposite picture can be depicted. In mentioning this aspect, a careful attention is required. In the table, Korean citizens marked high among the six nations surveyed on overall community service items. Koreans marked high especially high on items that are normative and less specific in nature and this tendency is reversed as the survey items are narrowed down to individual level ones that ask willingness for action. On item "I am willing to donate money to social service organization" and "I am willing to donate my internal organs", participation by the citizens in Korea has shrunken. This characteristic of the Korean citizens work as an undermining factor in maintaining civil society in the Korean context. People, while they are aware of normative values, they are hardly motivated when they are asked to participate at the individual level.

Conflict Resolution and Its Deeper Structure

Through the preceding section, this paper has presented how Korean society can be compared with other societies in terms of survey items that can constitute proxies for estimating social capital. As one reviews the results from the survey, an explicit observation is that Korean society has on the surface seems to have benign elements that can lead to the accumulation of social capital. On the other hand, those elements are rooted in such a way to work against the formation of social capital.

Then, a natural question would follow on what does the deficient social capital have to do with the realization of global standards in the public sector in Korea? A critical answer to this question comes from a notion that social capital is the soil or foundation from which all social relations can be established. More specifically, government activities are materialized in the settings of a specific society, and conditions of social capital would condition the environments in which those government activities can be exercised. Furthermore, it is crucial to acknowledge that activities o the government can be made when those activities are making contacts with the private sector. Thus, if certain conditions in the private sector feature degraded nature, it will be transferred to the public sector naturally. A consequence would be the low public sector performance and frustrations from citizens' side. In this context, the rule of game would be to "cheat", as would be exemplified in corruption cases. Also, all the efforts to improve the government would present only limited success, since the working environments are not favorable to the reform design.

Differences in the formation of civil society

Now, with the link between social capital and public sector performance, our focus should be given on what may be the cause for the low social capital in the Korean society that eventually reduced public sector performance.

3. Institutional Analysis and Its Contribution

Institutional analysis offers researchers referential frame works to compare different countries and different policies or combination of both. The advantages can be enhanced by institutional analysis' adoption of organization theories. In this essay, I will discuss how institutional analysis has been and can provide guidelines for comparison between countries or between policies. In other words, I will present what kinds of guidelines can be suggested by institutional analysis for policy transfers and institutional re-design. This chapter will first, review the notion of institutionalist theory of politics. Second, this section will assess the existing accumulation of institutionalist researches that are relevant for providing wisdom for policy transfers and institutional re-design.

Finally, I will suggest how can the findings be applied in other countries and other policy areas.

1) The notion of institutionalist theory of politics

Institutionalist theory of politics is a politics of how institutions bring stability and changes in a context of "democratic ideology". March and Olson present that institutional analysis studies an intermeshing of three system: the individual, the institution, and the environment. Although there are three variants of different institutionalisms, rational choice based institutionalism, historical institutionalism, and March and Olson's organizational theory based institutionalism, and they offer meaningful insights for policy borrowings, regarding about policy transfers and policy learnings, March and Olson type of institutional analysis is insighful. It is based on following grounds.

In March and Olson, organization theories are subset of institutional theory of politics, and they are building blocks of institutionalist theory in the sense that organization theory provides a variety of examples on how changes and stability of organizations actually occur. Furthermore, organization theory can offer a vehicle for comparison by providing "middle range theories" that facilitate comparative studies.

Then, based on the above notion, what is the institutionalist theory of politics? Before discussing the contributions and future applicability of institutionalist theory, I will present on this ,starting with the concept of institutions.

Depending on different camps of institutionalism, the

role and assumptions on institutions are defined and understood differently. They, however, seem to agree on the concept of the components of institutions. According to March and Olson, institutions can be understood as a set of rules, norms, standard operating procedures. They present that institutions are intermeshing of individuals, organizations, and environments. From Peter Hall, I can find similar definition; he argues that formal rules, compliance procedures, and standard operating procedures that structure the relationship between individuals in various units of the polity and economy as institutions.[94]

With the similar conception of institutions, authors in various institutionalism provide us theoretical developments on how institutions shape preferences and interests in the polity and economy or within the

---

94) Peter Hall, Governing the Economy: The Politics of State Intervention in Britain and France, oxford University Press. 1986. p.19
Katzenstein Between power and plenty: Foreign economic policies of advanced industrial states. University of Wisconsin Press.1978
Peter Evans, Skocpol, Theda. Et.al. eds. Bring the State back in. Cambridge University Press. 1985
Theda Skocpol, "Bringing the State Back In: Retrospect and Prospect", The 2007 Johan Skytte Prize Lecture. Scandinavian Political Studies, Volume31, Issue2, May 2008. Pages 109-124

contexts of institutionalist action. Thus, it is possible to say that institutionalist analysis, without denying the importance of both social context of politics and motives of individual actors, posits a more independent role for political institutions. For example, state is not only affected by society, but also affects it. (Katzenstein 1978, Skocpol 1979) In this context, political democracy depends not only on economic and social conditions, but also on the design of political institutions. Furthermore, bureaucracies, legislative committees, and courts are not only arenas for contending social interests, but also these institutions, which are collections of standard operating procedures and structures, define and defend values, norms interests, preferences, identities, and beliefs.

If I bring the focus to organizational level, following remarks can be made. Institutional analysis offers us to investigate the balance between societal forces and state bureaucracies.

In the next section, I will discuss contributions of institutionalist researches for policy transfers and institutional re-design. By policy transfers, I intend to understand a transfer between countries; by the concept of re-design, this section will discuss the implication available from institutional analysis performed in the U.S. for the re-design of future programs.

2) Contributions of institutional analysis for policy transfers and institutional re-design

Based on the discussion in the preceding sections, how institutional analysis of implementation and bureaucratic politics have offered implications. The reason I chose a focus on organization level institutional analysis is two-folded. First, bureaucracies are the "real" arenas where policies are implemented. Second, by focusing on the interactions between bureaucratic institutions and their environments, I can deduce implications for policy transfers and re-design of institutions.

2.1. Bureaucratic institutions and environments

Selznick's analysis of TVA shows how a public organization has adapted to and survived in its environments. Selznick shows with the concept of cooptation that how the agency absorbed outside interests into the organization to avert threats to existence and stability. Then, what was the relevance of cooptation in TVA case? TVA was a new organization as a conservation agency. The agency was intended to survive in the local settings with their original purposes, while at the same time they tried to have organizational autonomy vis a vis other branches of the federal government including the department of agriculture and the department of Interior. The way TVA took was to express its "grass roots ideology" as its protective ideology. With this ideology, TVA could formally coopt graa roots voluntary associations to acquire its legitimacy, and stand as the champion of local institutions.

TVA, on the other hand, was coopted by the farm lobby which exercised influence over TVA through "land grant college." One example of informal cooptation was the relationship between the lan grant college and te agricultural relations dept. of TVA; this relationship produced an absorption of strong centers of of interests in the valley area into policy determining structure of TVA. As a consequence of cooptation, TVA' fertilizer program. which was claimed to be TVA's grass roots procedures, was given to the representatives of conservative institutional forces, which biased the fertilizer program against poor farmers. In addition, TVA could not deal with the problem of farm tenancy, or the adjustment and re-location of poor farmers.

Furthermore, TVA's informal cooptation brought an unintended consequence. The new deal agricultural agencies like farm security administration and soil conservation service came under attack of the powerful American farm bureau federation, which thought that they would be threats to its access to farm population via "land grant colleges". Under the pressure of this farm interests, TVA could not recognize farm security administration and sought to exclude soil conservation service from operation in the "valley" area. It was a politically paradoxical phenomenon. TVA case shows that an agency, instead of acting as a reform agency, sought its survival. What the agency of TVA got from its interaction with its environments was that it was guaranteed its survival and support.

2.2. Lessons from Wildavsky and Pressman's Implementation

From Selznick's case, I can claim that bureaucracy's concerted efforts for its survival. In comparison, from the pioneering book, Implementation, one can argue for the complexity of joint actions in implementing governmental policies. In this sense, bureaucracies were faced with societal resistance in implementation. The authors presents how implementation of the EDA(Economic Development Administration) program went on in Oakland. The EDA, created by Congress, decided to go into cities to provide new permanent jobs to minorities. The intention of the EDA was to show how the provision of public works and building loans can provide incentives for employers to hire minorities.

Despite EDA's hope, however, the results in terms of minority employment were meager and disappointing. The authors draw some clues for these. First, creating a new agencies meant a less stable support grounds for the agency in its task environments. Second, the more the number of decision points, the less likelihood for the implementation of the program. Widavsky and Pressman point out the inverse relationship between the number of transactions required to implement a decision and the likelihood that an effect would result. Even when the probability of a favorable, intended result is high at each step like 0.9, the cumulative probability of transactions is extraordinarily low probability of success.[95] Third, we can infer from the book that wrong incentives were given to firms in a hope to increase minority employment. Capital subsidies to a firm building aircraft hangers were wrong incentives to guarantee minority employment; rather the firm should have given labor costs incentives, which is directly linked to the number of minority workers employed.

In comparison with TVA case, this study shows that organizations, especially new agencies needed strong support bases for its tasks. In addition, difference of environments between TVA's rural settings and EDA's

---

95) Richard Elmore, "Backward mapping: implementation research and policy decisions, political science quarterly, vol.94 number 4, winter 1979-1980

urban settings bring us difficulty of EDA to expand its support bases easily. With these difficulties. EDA carried out its tasks, although tangentially influenced. Despite the notion that individual agencies struggled in its task environments in both TVA and EDA cases, what can be claimed is that Bureaucracy had a such staying power to resist environments and joint decision problems that they eventually achieved some portion of their goals. But this is not to say that EDA's projects were successful implementation; authors in the first part of the book clearly say that it is wrong to attribute relative damage of Oakland area during the riots in 1968 to the projects of EDA. [96] The aim and contribution of the book was that it showed implementation is another stage of continuous decision making process, and not an automated process where legislature's and bureaucracies' original intentions are served completely.

---

96) Jeffery L.Pressman and Aaron Wildavsky, implementation, p.xix

2.3. Bureaucratic politics as an institutional politics

Politics in the bureaucracy is another contribution of institutionalist theory in exercising policy transfers and re-design of institutions. Prof. Sapolsky's brilliant book, The Polaris system development, clearly shows how proponents of a program manuervered within the bureaucracy to have their desired plan to be enacted and then how they made their efforts to protect the program in progress as they intended.

The FBM(missile) proponents had two objectives: one was to gain approval for the solid fueled ballistic missile for submarine launch and to get the degree of organizational autonomy within the navy. Through the science advisory committee, the proponents could circumvent bureaucratic hierarchy; thus, the proponents could deduce the necessity to rely on the top decision level for the polaris missile by bypassing the hierarchy.

The book presented that the proponents of the program adopted four bureaucratic strategies to protect the program: differenciation, co-optation, moderation, and myth from managerial techniques. The crucial point is not that the proponents adopted the strategies. The success required skills in using bureaucratic politics. The very value of the book lies in the fact that it showed how bureaucratic politics worked.

2.4. Deregulation case

My fourth example of institutionalist politics for getting implications for the policy transfers comes from the deregulation case in the U.S. Policy ideas for the deregulation, which was picked up by politicians and supported by "neutral intellectuals."[97] Through a very complex processes of interactions between business interests, Congress, and the administration, the deregulation bill was passed. The idea that deregulation itself can bring economic benefits inspired plenty of countries to adopt the policy idea in the 1980s.

2.5. Veto points argument

Professor Immergut[98] offers an argument that provides a clue for national divergence, given the other conditions equal. In her comparative case study, interests of doctors, interest groups, and the state's

---

97) Derthick, Martha, and Paul J. Quirk. The politics of deregulation. Brookings Institution Press, 2001.
98) Immergut, Ellen M. Health politics: interests and institutions in Western Europe. CUP Archive, 1992.

intention were identical, and thereby could be treated as constants. With this treatment, net effects of institutions could be investigated. Depending on whether interest groups could access to veto points or not, policy outcomes were different. Following this argument, one can know that re-design of national level institutions would bring crucial differences.

3) Possibilities of transferring policies and re-design of institutions

In this part, based on the preceding sections, I will discuss whether the contributions of institutionalist theories can be applied in policy transfers and the re-design of institutions.

Several points can be presented on policy transfers. First, difficulties of implementation are found in other countries as well. Thus, implementation difficulties and literatures on this can be transferred to other countries. Possible differences between Wildavsky's case and other countries would depend on bureaucratic capacity including the degree of centralization.

In the case of the "new community movement" in Korea from 1960s to 1980s, instead of being co-opted, the field agencies boostered competition between rural communities. In that sense, TVA's implications were used in designing institutions and policies. But the problem in this case was that it was later on so politicized that it collapsed when the administration was changed. Thus, it failed to create regional linkages, as were in the TVA case.

Second, there are a lot of policy learning on "deregulation" in other countries. However, differences of domestic policy making institutional arrangements would make it difficult for other countries have deregulation measures in the same way as the U.S. Although there would be deregulation, the mode or the type of deregulation would dependent on national characterisitcs.

Third, I would like to mention the limitations of policy transfers. If any institutional analysis was done in the case study method, then it would be difficult to have generalization. In this context, transferring the findings in to a foreign country and expecting the same results would be risky. Another factor that would hamper the policy transfer is cultural factors.

Fourth, another danger of policy transfer is the danger of "formalism". Empirically, Korean government imported budgetary techniques from the U.S. PPBS(planning, programing, budgeting system) and ZBB(zero based budget) were two of many examples. The result of these imports, according to one official in the bureau, was that there has been high possibility of having "formalism" in the sense that original meaning is not transferred from "inventing country". If the reform was in the rethoric, then policy transfer would be meaningless. In other words, it takes time until new institution take roots.

Fifth, in terms of re-designing institutions, institutionalist theory can contribute in two ways. One is through the accumulation of organization theories. These theories can be transferred to other countries with consideration of specific conditions in other countries. For example, using matrix structure in the R&D oriented institutions can be neutrally transferred to other countries. This case would be less affected by cultural, and other institutional aspects. The other way of contribution is inferred from a case from France. In this case, after changing Constitutions, the country cleared the practice of cycling of votes in the legislative body. Thus, in investigating a country's bureaucratic capacity, the country can have strong capacity in absolute terms compared to other countries, and yet can not exercise it in policy formulation at the legislative body. It can be explained by the differences of voting and veto system. With this insight, one designer of a Constitution can design a bureaucracy with more penetrative power vis a vis society; or he can restrain bureaucracy from the beginning.

Chapter 4

Paradigm Shifts in Social Science

1. Prologue

Thomas Kuhn's idea of scientific revolution has influenced various disciplines both in natural sciences and social sciences. Although these two areas of disciplines are affected, the impact and the implications of the scientific revolutions and paradigm shifts that followed had different meanings. In natural sciences, for example in physics, when a new paradigm by Einstein appears, the new paradigm was developed in a way to contain the old paradigm of Newtonian physics.

In contrast, in social sciences, truly multiple paradigms co-exist in the identical time frame, and paradigm shift is very difficult to accomplish. Despite this difference, in this essay, I will try to present how paradigm shift has occurred in political science by utilizing two paradigms; systems theory(which bases on biology) and Statism(which bases on Weberian tradition). With these two paradigms, the policy question I am focusing on is how a political system and its outcomes(policies) can be explained.

In answering this question, I will first present the two paradigms on their core assumptions, heuristics with which the paradigm develops its theory, empirical evidences and means of persuasion, together with exemplars in the paradigms. Then, I will discuss why the paradigm shift has occurred. Finally, I will discuss the peculiarities of social science paradigms at the end.

2. The Old Paradigm: The Systems theory By David Easton

1) The core assumptions & Proposition

David Easton's aim in establishing his theory was to

build a general model of understanding the state. He believed that every society has similar functions, which can be analyzed in a common analytical framework.

(Core Assumptions)

In building his theory, Easton borrowed his reference framework from biology.[99] Thus, core assumptions in his theory resembles the assumptions used in biology, which are followings. First, a society, as a living system should satisfy its basic needs and functional requirements. This is expressed by using biological concepts such as equilibrium or homeostasis. Second, in his model building, such biological concepts as, environments, boundaries were used to describe the political system. Each societal element has one to one match with components in David Easton model.

(Heuristics)

In Lakatos's view, a positive heuristic is an entity that a research program is assumed to be progressed by

---

99) David Easton, A Framework for Political Analysis, Prentice Hall. 1965.

resorting to it; the heuristic contains hard core values, including those contained in assumptions, and helps research programs to develop theories that contain the core values.[100)]

In David Easton model, followings can be presented as positive heuristics of the model. First, since there is a functional requirement that any system, should it survive, should maintain equilibrium, inputs level is regulated by the gatekeeper, which is an analog of the interest groups. Second, similar in vein, inputs that come from society are only demands and support, rather than opposition to the system. Third, to fulfill his aim to cover all the variants of political systems, the political system is simplified as a black box; this is theoretically backed in the sense that David Easton had an assumption that any society has similar functions, and need not want to know about the dynamics in the political system.

With the simplified model of political system, outputs are policies which go to society. There are

---

100) Diesing, Paul. How does social science work?: Reflections on practice. University of Pittsburgh Press, 1992. chapter 2.

cybernetic communications between society and the political system.

(Induction and deduction)

In building his theory, Easton relied first on induction to use biological metaphors to match with real world political systems. Then, he used deductions to develop his theory further and tried to develop testable hypotheses.

(Persuasiveness and evidence)

A paradigm, to be successful, should be proved empirically, and also persuade scientific community. Kuhn's scientific revolution, in this sense, reflects sociology of scientific community.[101] David Easton model as a paradigm that embodies biological metaphors had following persuasiveness and empirical evidences to be supported as a successful paradigm.

First, his theory seems to reflect the real world politics, especially that of the U.S. U.S. politics was

---

101) Thomas Kuhn, The Structure of scientific Revolutions 1962.

already disaggregated and was dominated by the interest groups[102], and thus the state or in a more reduced terminology the political system was an arena of competing interests, which eventually treated in Easton model as a black Box, inside of which should not be known.

Second, the model of systems theory was easy to understand, and therefore was able to persuade more audience.

Third, related to the political and economic situations of the 1950s and 1960s, his theory became even more popular. In the advanced countries, convergence theories began supporting an ideal dream of the affluent societies, and Easton model was the model that could be dreamed of.[103] In this period, in

---

102) Morone, James A. The democratic wish: Popular participation and the limits of American government. Yale University Press, 1998.
 Lowi, T. J. (1969). The end of liberalism: Ideology, policy, and the crisis of public authority.
 Gourevitch, Peter Alexis. Politics in hard times: Comparative responses to international economic crises. Cornell University Press, 1986.
103) Joint Committee on Western Europe. Order and conflict in contemporary capitalism. Ed. John H. Goldthorpe. Oxford: Clarendon Press, 1984., chapter 13 on convergence

Europe, Keynesian demand management policies boostered business confidence that business cycles can now be controlled,[104) and this ensured further investment , which led to a boom.

Similarly, with regard to the relevance to developing countries, his theory could still make claims that it can cover variations of the third world countries.

Fourth, in academic sense, the development of the discipline of biology helped Easton model to be more persuasive. It was the time when DNA was discovered. In social science, a general trend toward behavioralism de-emphasized the observation of the state side, and then claimed that observable societal sides can produce meaningful results[105).

Fifth, David Easton model was a paragon for generalization in social sciences, which was useful in

---

104) Boltho, Andrea, and Barry Eichengreen. "The economic impact of European integration." (2008).
    Boltho, A., & Glyn, A. (1995). Can macroeconomic policies raise employment. Int'l Lab. Rev., 134, 451.

105) Steinmo, Sven, Kathleen Thelen, and Frank Longstreth, eds. Structuring politics: historical institutionalism in comparative analysis. Cambridge University Press, 1992. chapter 1
    Gabriel Almond, "Return to the State," American Political Science Review, vol 82. no.3 Sept .1988.

international relations studies. Sixth, it was believed that ,by pursuing generalization in systems theory, scholars should now no longer rely on "history" elements to explain.[106]

Exemplars are examples that can be used to disseminate the paradigm. In this context, David Easton's own book, A Framework for political analysis, was an excellent example.

3. The New Paradigm

The new paradigm against the biology based paradigm came in the name of the return to the State, which reflected the dissatisfaction of the old paradigm. In this section, while I explain the new paradigm, I will try to incorporate the part on why this transition happened.

---

106) Theda Skocpol, Bringing the State back in. *op.cit.*

1) Core assumptions

Above all, scholars in the new paradigm objects the idea that political system can be reduced to a back box. The state is an autonomous entity rather than a dependent variable and an arena.[107]   Second, in this new paradigm, historical legacy and contingency takes an important part, compared to ahistorical approach of the systems theory. What a society or a political system chose as an option impacts the track of the system in the future; furthermore, with the autonomy of the state, state as an actor can chose at its best interests. Thus, equilibrium is not a virtue any more, on the contrary, state is the agent of change.

2) Positive Heuristics

In developing theoretical approach, the new paradigm of statism applied the core concept of the state. In

---

107) Theda Skocpol, Bringing the State back in. *op.cit*

using this, a compromise was made in order to facilitate cross national comparison; the compromise was due from the difficulty of defining the term state. In treating the state, researchers used bureaucracy as a middle range framework that facilitated comparison.

Historically, it was proven that whenever revolutions occur, what revolutionaries first did was to take control of the bureaucracy as a machine, which will follow its new "master". In other cases, creating a new bureaucracy was an alternative to this. Another historical evidence was from Crane Brinton's Analysis of the revolutions,[108] in which he claimed that as long as bureaucracies are not fell down to "decay groups", i.e. as long as the decay groups(revolutionaries) are not infiltrated in the bureaucracy, the political system is safe from revolution. An implication from this is that the bureaucracy is the backbone to the state.

As heuristics, other useful concepts as strong state -- weak state and business government consultation were used to develop the whole notion of the state as an actor.

---

108) Brinton, Crane. "The anatomy of revolution." (1938).

3) Examples

The next stage of developing a paradigm utilizing heuristic came in several forms.

(Strong state vs. weak state)

Peter Katzenstein [109]argued that strong states in Europe and Japan has contributed to the superior economic performance of these countries.

(Business--Government relations)

Numerous researches have been conducted in this tradition. Richard Samuel, Marie Anchordougie wrote on Japanese government and business consultation modes. Alice Amsden on Korean and Taiwan cases and Robert Wade'[110]s contribution also illuminated how state side can be used to illuminate the economic growth processes of these countries.

---

109) Peter Katzenstein, Between power and Plenty 1978.
110) Amsden, Alice Hoffenberg. Asia's next giant: South Korea and late industrialization. Oxford University Press, USA, 1992.

Wade, Robert. Governing the market: Economic theory and the role of government in East Asian industrialization. Princeton University Press, 2004.

4) Why did Paradigm shift occurred?

To have a paradigm shift, there should be empirical evidences to disprove the existing old paradigm as well as persuasive power of the new paradigm. As I have mentioned briefly in the early part of this essay, social science paradigms do not change like the paradigms in natural sciences. In a similar vein, in this essay, I will show how different alternative approaches jointly undermined the existing paradigm, while providing empirical evidences and persuasiveness of the new paradigm.

(Deficiencies of the systems theory I)

In the late 1970s, it seemed evident that dreams of convergence and endless growth were falling apart. Against the identical external schlock of oil shock, however, outcomes of economic policies began diverging across countries. Thus, to capture this divergence, no longer it is possible to rely on a common model.

It was this context that Statism as exemplified by

Katzenstein's strong state argument or Mancur Olson's The Rise and Fall of nations began to receive attention, because they seemed to provide alternative models that can explain the divergence. Only difference was that while Olson built his theory from micro level foundations, focusing on whether interest groups are facilitated or not, to macro level economic performance, Katzenstein merely used the metaphor of the strong state.

(Deficiency II)

In connection with the above deficiency that induced the shift of paradigm, it is possible to mention a more fundamental problem in methodological sense; the debate on generalization through an universal model vs. individualization through middle range comparison.

Both approaches aimed eventually at drawing out meaningful comparison. Backed by the scientific community that could not support the universal model such as the systems theory, the new paradigm could get more persuasion.

(Deficiency III)

The borrowed model of systems theory were faced with problems of external validity. Simply, there was no 1 to 1 match to the real world phenomenon. Furthermore, it was empirically proved that societies would not behave in equilibrium. As an alternative societies may behave in a long cycle of growth and death. Sociologists and other political scientists provided theoretical grounds for this argument.

Samuel Huntington claimed that it is the responsibility of the elite that caused the government overload in the U.S, since people do not know how to balance their demands. Not only in the US., but also in many developed nations, such as Italy in 1968, France in 1968, demands of people seemed to have no satisfaction.[111] Thus, Easton model's validity was ever weakening with these empirical evidences.

In addition, researches on interests formation showed

---

111) Huntington, Samuel P. "The democratic distemper." The Public Interest 41 (1975): 9.
Berger, Suzanne. "Organizing interests in Western Europe: Pluralism, corporatism, and the transformation of politics." Cambridge University Press. 1983.

that interests formation is far more complex than Easton had thought, and it is influenced by historical alliances.

Together with above factors, the old paradigm began losing its grounds. In the next section, I will bring an issue of the characteristics of social sciences in terms of paradigm shift as a concluding remark.

4.Paradigm shifts in social sciences

As I have stated above, in social sciences, rather than having a complete paradigm shift, there are multiplicity of competing paradigms as new paradigms enter into the academic arena. Or another possible view is that as a new paradigm enters, the old paradigm becomes a degenerating paradigm.

In case of degenerating paradigms, following Lakatos and Feryerabend's suggestions, I think it is better to give the failing paradigm a new chance to produce meaningful contributions to science.

In the case of David Easton model, although it is reduced in its status as a prime model for exploiting the frontier of science, it is still an useful exemplar for pedagogical purposes at schools. It is still easy to understand and easy to persuade laymen in a different context. In comparison, the new paradigm of statism has many weaknesses to overcome and establish itself as a dominant paradigm. In a very absolute standard, most of social science paradigms are in the pre-paradigmatic stages.

What brings this peculiarity of social sciences? In my view, one of the reasons is the lack of common yard stick to compare different paradigms in social sciences, other than persuasiveness of the theory and metaphors the theory incorporates. This reason brings limitations to use paradigm schema in social sciences, while the paradigm oriented thinking really contributed in understanding the theory development and the sociology of sciences in general.

1) *Metaphors of Mathematics*

Mathematics is a language in establishing a theory, and thereby constructing a lens to view social phenomenon. Mathematics can be analogued as a building block for building a theory and in this sense there is no difference in theory building, when compared to other areas of theory building.

The mathematics has, however, multiple facets, which means there exists different mathematics that are utilized in theory building in social sciences.

In this essay, first, I will present how different mathematics are used in different sub-disciplines of social sciences. Secondly, I will focus on optimization and iterated functional systems to show implications from these theories.

2) Different Languages of Mathematics in Social sciences

Classical Economics :optimization, equilibrium

Classical economics was modeled after the classical physics of the 19th century. Since then, classical theory and its successor neo-classical theory did not update the mathematics, while physics showed a dramatic departure from the 19th century level.

As a result of borrowing models. classical economics was exactly patterned after the classical physics. Instead of the balances of forces, now markets clear; instead of the notion that time is absolutely separate from space, money is separate from market. In this sense, money was regarded as a veil.

In formulating an economic model, classical economics was based on methodological individualism, and for its mathematical part, it relied on marginal "revolution that occurred in the 19th century. The downward sloping of individual demand curve is based on diminishing marginal utility of the product and marshallian condition that the marginal utility of money income is constant.[112]

On the producers' side. there was a principle of diminishing marginal productivity. In theorizing in economics, Kapital(K) and Labor (L) were selected as production factors.

With these classical economics could be summarized by a total production function, conditions for profit maximization, labor supply curve, and Marshall's quantity theory of money. In this framework, "optimization" provided a tool to analyze such phenomenon as utility maximization and profit maximization. Maximization and minimization principles are also utilized in the analysis of oligopolistic markets and monopoly markets.

Equilibrium analysis also contributed to the development of classical economics. In a typical Walrusian general equilibrium, we can find assumptions of perfect information and no uncertainty. In this, Walrus contributed by suggesting a system of analyzing

---

112) Gerald T. Garvey a, Peter L. Swan., "The economics of corporate governance: Beyond the Marshallian firm", Journal of Corporate Finance. Volume 1, Issue 2, August 1994, Pages 139-174

all markets, commodity markets and production factor markets, at the same time. For example, he showed that to know the quantity demanded for x, one needs to know not only the price of x, but also prices of other goods and the prices of other production factors that were used in the production of those goods.

Optimization example II: management techniques

Optimization is widely applied in linear programming, queuing, and other management techniques. These math models are basically prescriptive in nature, and very micro in scope. Also these math models always leave a question of external validity, i.e. whether the model has realistic aspects.

Game Theory

Game theory usually assumes a hypothetical "game situation". The players in the game have assumptions on their behaviors. The simple form of game theory starts with 2 person non-iterative game situations, such as prisoners' dilemma.

The mathematical backgrounds for game theory is found from the micro economics where optimization methods are used. As the models become complicated in game theories, typical forms include n-person game theory. But the core ideas are based on the deductions from the situations and strategies that players are faced with.

Iterated functional systems

In the field such as chaos theory, iterated functions provide useful means of mathematical tools. Compared to the static world of mathematics where optimization principles are applied, this "newly found math in social sciences offer a new possibility to look at a phenomenon with an expanded time frame, and to discover the underlying possible sub-structure that we did not think of.

Especially with the concept and mechanics of the "punctuated equilibrium", in explaining evolution or other dramatic cumulative changes, it is possible to draw out useful implications.

3) Implications from the Different Schools of Math

In the preceding section, I have briefly discussed on different mathematics in social sciences. One interesting point to discuss is that from these different math, we glean different implications that are useful and meaningful in our analysis. In this section, specifically focusing on optimization world and iterated functions & punctuated equilibrium world, I will present how we, as researchers, can apply these new methods.

Implications from the math of the punctuated equilibrium

Despite the elegant development of the standard classical economics, researchers find frustrations when they are faced with constraints that are not realistic. For example, in neo-classical economics, there is not much room for technological change, which is a major force that changes fundamentally in our society.

Theoretically (not in math), we have enjoyed an alternative to this neo-classical economics, the Schumpeterian economics of social change. In my view, we did not have math to actually implement the theory. In Schumpeterian vision, the development of capitalism is a creative destruction[113], in which the existing structures, including social structures, are destroyed. By utilizing punctuated equilibrium model, it becomes possible to see this dynamic. Prior to this usage of punctuated equilibrium model, in my view, if a researcher wants to research social mobility change due from industrialization, Markov model was an alternative. Instead of this, Punctuated equilibrium model brings a bigger picture.

In a more generic sense, the model of punctuated equilibrium can be linked to the analysis of "evolution". Not only pure phenomenon of evolution, but also any phenomenon that has "evolution like" traits can be approached through this math; one example can be a study on the new niches of a product or a research on market segment change & competition between different brands still utilizing biological metaphors.

---

113) Schumpeter, Joseph A. Capitalism, socialism and democracy. routledge, 2013.

Implications from other math

From the traditional optimization math, we can still get a snapshot of a phenomenon. In this area also, I think there would be more usage of the math in refining what we have been doing in this area.

5. Concluding Remark

Mathematics clearly is a language, by which one can develop and establish a theoretical framework. It has beautiful mathematical properties that can be tested and repeated. In this sense, it is an advanced step toward scientification of social sciences. There is no doubt on the point that this effort should be continued.

But there exists one caution. Like math is a language, math based theory should also be tested like non math based theories in social sciences. This includes tests of external validity and persuasion. With these points in mind, mathematics will contribute as a language in the theory development in social sciences.

Chapter 5

Policy Issues

1. Prologue

Defense technology development has been faced with key issues since recent several decades.[114] While different schools of thought may differ in the relative importance of the details, it may be feasible to distill the key issues, as rising R&D requirements and budget constraints,[115] increased pressure on the

---

114) Stowsky, Jay. (1996) "The dual-use dilemma: technologies for commercial and military applications", Issues in Science and Technology Vol.13, Issue no.2. National Academy of Sciences, pp.56-64.
James, Andrew. (2006) "US Defence R&D Spending: An Analysis of the Impacts",
James, Andrew. (2006) "The transatlantic defence R&D gap: causes, consequences and controversies", Defence and Peace Economics, Vol.17, No.3, 2006: pp. 223-238.

115) Glass, Robert. (2002) Facts and Fallacies of Software Engineering, Addison-Wesley, New York, NY.Brooks, Frederick. (1995) The Mythical Man-Month: Essays on Software Engineering, 20th Anniversary Edition, Addison-Wesley Professional,

sensitivity to the socio economic values for investment, and unresolved answer to the Spin-off vs. Spin-on debate.[116] Under these circumstances, in developing and fostering cutting edge defense related technologies, it is a clear trend to eye on dual use technology track.[117] This chapter, taking this as a backdrop, tried to approach the issue by examing whether inter displinary research can assist the promotion of dual use technology development. In so doing, this research first reviewed traditional and more recent inter displinary approaches to dual use

---

New York, NY

116) Branscomb, Alic J., L., Brooks, H., Carter, A. and Epstein, G. (1992). Beyond Spinoff: Military and Commercial Technologies in a Changing World, Harvard Business School Press, Boston.
Stowsky, Jay. (1992) "From Spin-off to Spin-On: Redefining the Military's Role in American Technological Development," in Wayne Sandholtz et al, The Highest Stakes: The Economic Foundations of the Next Security System. New York, Oxford University Press, pp. 114-140.
James, Andrew, Cox, D and Rigby, J. (2005) "Testing the boundaries of Public-Private Partnership: the privatisation of the UK Defence Evaluation & Research Agency", Science & Public Policy, 32 (2), April: pp.155-161.

117) Bellais, Renaud and Guichard, Renelle. (2006) "Defense Innovation, technology transfers and Public Policy", Defence and Peace Economics, Volume 17, Number 3, June. pp. 273-286. Molas-Gallart, Jordi. (1997) "Which way to go? Defence technology and the diversity of 'dual-use' technology transfer", Research Policy Volume 26, Issue 3, October 1997, pp. 367-385.

technology development, followed by an empirical analysis to link the relationship between investment in inter displinary research and outcomes, in which outcomes are proxied values for potential dual use technology development in the new trend. Implications suggest that promoting inter displinary research can be a viable option in promoting dual use technology development.

2. Traditional approach to Dual Use Technology Development

Through history, military technology has been the cutting edge area for any country in any conceivable time frame.[118] It is, therefore, not a surprising fact in history that a super power nation of the century or the era had possessed an unmatching military superiority

---

118) Kim, Junmo. (2002) "Network building between research institutions and small & medium enterprises(SMEs): dynamics of innovation network building and implications for a policy option", International Journal of Technology, Policy and Management (IJTPM) Vol. 2. No.3. Winter. pp.272-285

from technology side. War has produced, in this sense, a swarm of new technologies that have been used after wars. A critical drawback in maintaining this technological edge has been that development costs have been sky rocketing, which has been intensified through the 20th century.

A very natural course of action has been to rely on dual use technology development, since technology has been understood as a source of economic growth.[119] In this setting, the notion of spin-off has come into the setting. It is needless to list all the beautiful arguments that have supported the spin-off argument, because there are too many and they are so well refined. The most fundamental contest that the spin-off argument had to go through has been how much contribution can actually be assigned to dual use technology development for economic growth.[120] While theory has been elegant,

119) Solow, Robert. (1956) "A Contribution to the Theory of Economic Growth", The Quarterly Journal of Economics, 70(1), 65-94.
120) Cowan, R. and Foray, D. (1995) "Quandaries in the economics of dual technologies and spillovers from military to civilian research and development", Research Policy 24, pp. 851–868.

proving what has been done has not been easy.

Spin-on argument came as a savior to dual use technology development, yet the philosophy behind it is quite opposite to the spin-off paradigm. Emphasizing spin-on would mean promoting private sector initiatives, rather than presenting government-led visions. Successful stories of Japan and Sweden can clearly demonstrate the efficacy of the spin-on argument. These countries, while faithful on their economic development and technological pursuit, could quite naturally be endowed with capabilities that could be utilized in military uses in the name of COTs (commercial off-the-shelf technologies.[121]) Against the spin-off vs. spin-on debate, contexts for dual use development has been intensifie

---

121) Fong, Gwenda. (2004) "Adapting cots games for military simulation", VRCAI "04: *Proceedings of the 2004 ACM SIGGRAPH international conference on Virtual Reality continuum and its applications in industry.* June
Demko, E.(1996) "Commercial-off-the shelf (COTS): a challenge to military equipment reliability", *Reliability and Mantainability Symposium*, 1996 Proceedings. "International Symposium on Product Quality and Integrity". Vol.: 22-25 Jan. pp.7 - 12
Li, Jingyue, Finn Olav Bjørnson, Reidar Conradi and Vigdis B. Kampenes. (2006) "An empirical study of variations in COTS-based software development processes in the Norwegian IT industry", *Empirical Software Engineering* Volume 11, Number 3 September.

d[122)] in the sense that most dual use technology fields have been so interwound that no single area can be established without mingling with neighboring and non-neighboring fields.[123)]

3. Interdisplinary Approach to Dual Use Technology Development : A Background

While spin-off strategy to defense related technology development would be remaining as one of the core pillar, several key developments have occurred during recent three decades that have been urging a watershed in defense related development.

First, as in other technology fields, technology

---

122) Molas-Gallart, Jordi. (1997) "Which way to go? Defence technology and the diversity of 'dual-use' technology transfer", *Research Policy* Volume 26, Issue 3, October 1997, pp. 367-385.
123) Kim, Junmo. (2007)a "Will Technology Fusion induce the Paradigm Change of University Education?" International Journal of Technology Management (IJTM) Vol. 38., no.3. pp.220-234.

components in most defense related projects have become more complex, which can easily be linked to increased budget requirements (Reifer 2004). In fighter development case, the ratio of software part has increased substantially over the 50 year period,[124] which has turned the aerospace business from a traditional airframe manufacturer to a complex integration industry that is composed of electronics and all the existing components of aerospace sector.[125]

Another reason why budget has skyrocketed comes from the changing nature of defense duties. Very similar to health sector, defense sector has been transformed in to a sector that desires to save friendly and even hostile lives as long as military objectives can be attained. As seen from the Gulf war in 1991 and

---

124) Glass, Robert. (2002) *Facts and Fallacies of Software Engineering*, Addison-Wesley, New York, NY.
Winter, Don C. (1996) "Modular, Reusable Flight Software For Production Aircraft", 15thAIAA/IEEE Digital Avionics Systems Conference Proceedings, October, pp. 401-406.
125) Amorelli, T. (1996) "Dual use and technology transfer in the titanium industry", IPTS Report 4, pp. 27–30.
Brooks, Frederick. (1995) *The Mythical Man-Month*: Essays on Software Engineering, 20th Anniversary Edition, Addison-Wesley Professional, New York, NY.

other recent conflicts, war captives and injuries bring added stress to political leaders. One viable way to overcome this comes from a more capital intensive military forces based on technological superiority, which implies more capital intensive development requirements. This has been identical in health sector in many advanced nations.[126] Unless there is a will in political sphere to contain medical costs increase, capital has replaced labor. In other words, as long as budget can be supplied, new equipment could save lives and saved lives could be regarded as the achievements and ways to remove blames for not able to cure diseases. All these have added up budget requests for equipment that was previously done at an efficient way.

Second, while one can still argue for the efficacy of spin-off strategy, the actual impact from spin offs can hardly be materialized in the short term.[127] In extreme

126) Sapolsky, Harvey M.(1992) *Comparing Health and Defense.* MIT Center for International Studies (CIS), Cambridge, September.

127) Carr, R.K. (1994) "Doing technology transfer in federal laboratories", in: Suleiman, K. and Radosevich, R., Editors. *From Lab to Market. Commercialization of Public Sector Technology,* Plenum Press, New York, pp. 61–87

cases, the effect of spin offs may be materialized in a foreign country rather than in the mother country of the technology as evidenced by Japanese consumer electronics sector with examples of micro wave oven and others.

Third, in defense fields, as would be similar in other cases, a phenomenon of technology integration has been occurring in many different cases. Today, a new defense technology item is not a single product composed of one technology. Even in a vehicle or a unit product, knowledge requirements have been increasing, following new demands in the field. This can be interpreted as increased necessity to rely on interdisplinary research basis.

Against these changing contexts, a clearly observable development was to emphasize dual use technology development. Dual use approach, however, is clearly a neutral way in the sense that this lofty dual use idea can be approached from either spin-off or spin-on direction. If dual use development is approached from a spin-off way, then it may be arguably clear that the existing problem from the traditional spin-off approach would not be resolved. Highly rising costs and interrelated nature of new technologies can make the realization of spin-off effect in private economy a more remote and far-away dream.

Understanding the notion of interdisplinary research

While most advanced nations share a lot of science & technology related issues including defense related and dual use technology issues, countries differ in their needs to accept or change their positions regarding dual use and spin off strategy. The U.S. obviously have decisive advantage in the sense that resources including research expenditures have been abundant vis-à-vis other European countries. This difference has alerted European countries open their eyes on COTs earlier than the U.S. in general.[128] COTs, in some sense, has not proved to

---

128) Hall, J. and Naff, R. (2000) "The cost of COTS" Digital Avionics Systems Conferences, Proceedings, October. 7th-13th. Volume: 1, pp. 4B1/1-4B1/6. Philadelphia, PA, USA Kline, Ronald R. and Thomas C. Lassman. (2005) "Competing Research Traditions in American Industry: Uncertain Alliances between Engineering and Science at Westinghouse Electric, 1886–1935", Journal : Enterprise Soc., Dec. vol.6. pp.601 - 645

be an omni potent solution yet, since custom designed products may prove to be more cost effective in military senses.[129] Aviation and naval shipbuilding areas have reported either increased life cycle costs or improper functioning of the COTs, which signals the effectiveness of the traditional approach, non-COTs, to defense technology acquisition.[130] From the drawback, however, what can be inferred from is that more interdisplinary components are needed, and COTs could be regarded as a middle ground and a bridging tool in entering interdisplinary fields,[131] since COTs imply that

129) McGraw, G. and J. Viega. (1999) "Why COTS Software Increases Security Risks" ICSE Workshop on Testing Distributed Component-Based Systems, May 1999.
Voas, J. (1998)a "A Defensive Approach to Testing Systems that Contain COTS and Third-Party Functionality In the Proceedings AQUIS '98, Venice, April 1998

130) Alford, Lionel Jr.(1999) "The Problem With Aviation Cots - commercial off the shelf purchasing", *Acquisition Review Quarterly*, Summer.
Alford, Lionel Jr. (2001) "The Problem with Aviation Cots", *IEEE Aerospace & electronics Systems Magazine* Febuary. pp.33-37.
Benguria, Gorka, Ana Belén , David Sellier, and Sandy Tay. (2002) "European COTS User Working Group: Analysis of the Common Problems and Current Practices of the European COTS Users", *Lecture Notes in Computer Science*, Volume 2255. pp.44-53.

131) Voas, J. (1998)b. "COTS software: The economical choice?", *IEEE Software*, vol. 15, no.2. pp.16 -19.
Kim, Junmo. (2007)a "Will Technology Fusion induce the Paradigm Change of University Education?" International

similar solutions can be found commonly from other areas. In this sense, it is a step forward from traditional dual use concept. In sum, while COTS can be seen as a step forward in the lineage of dual use approach, using COTS amplifies the need for interdisplinary research.

Even in the shared understanding of the necessity to emphasize interdisplinary research following the changing environments, the U.S. and European nations presented a subtle difference in accepting the notion of interdisplinary fields[132] or technology convergence areas.

Journal of Technology Management (IJTM) Vol. 38., no.3. pp.220-234.

132) Evered. (2004) "Research in the behavioural and social sciences to improve cancer control and care: a strategy for development", *European Journal of Cancer* Volume 40, Issue 3 February pp.316-325.
Philip , K. L., K. Backett-Milburn, S. Cunningham-Burley, and J. B. Davis. (2003) "Practising what we preach? A practical approach to bringing research, policy and practice together in relation to children and health inequalities", Health Education Research., Oct. vol.18, pp.568 - 579.
Blake, M.B. (2005) "Integrating large-scale group projects and software engineering approaches for early computer science courses", *IEEE Transactions on Education*, Feb. Volume: 48, Issue: 1. pp.63- 72.

	Common point	Difference
Multi-displinary Cross-displinary	Academic displines of A and B are joined.	After certain period, A and B will go back to the original position. Problem is resolved.
Interdisplinary stage		While a problem is resolved, discipline A and B are amalgamed into a new discipline C.

Table 2 Concept of interdisplinary research

	United States	E.U.
Definition	Convergence of Nano-Bio-Info-Cognitive fields	Enabling technology that opens possibilities to different fields
Scope	Nano-Bio-Info-Cognitive fields	Including Humanities and Social Sciences in addition to emerging science fields
Major Characteristics	- NSF has a leading role - Not specifying exact fields - Recommendations for business, government, and academia for potentials	- designating 5major fields of health, education, informatics, energy, and environment - natural language, curing obesesity, and intellectual housing environment as proposed examples

Table 3 Comparison of the notion of interdisplinary fields

In the U.S. based on documentation from various sources, it is reasonable to present the contents in table. While the U.S. and EU share a notion that NBIC are major fields for interdisplinary research, EU added humanities and social science fields as examples of interdisplinary areas. EU has designated 5 areas where interdisplinary research is promising, in contrast to the U.S. approach not to specify the fields. Despite the difference, however, in both U.S. and EU, it is possible to present academic and policy cases, which can be presented in the below.

Cases from the U.S., EU and Japan

The U.S. cases

The U.S., in fact, has been a forerunner in creating and practicing interdisplinary fields.[133] Starting from the Media Lab in late 1980s and early 1990s, MIT has

---

133) *Inside Higher Education* "Institutionalizing' Interdisciplinary Research" July 25th, 2007

established the STAT center in 2004 to facilitate neuroscience field. This could be understood as a continuing effort of brain research that has been undertaken since the media lab was established. Also noteworthy in the STAT case is that it is clearly benefited from geographically adjacent institutions including Harvard University, Mass general hospital and other significant players in brain research in New England region.

Another U.S. example comes from Stanford's BIO-X project, in which engineering, computer, physics, and chemical fields are interwound into Biology field.

The European and Japanese cases

As hinted from the table 2 in the above, Europe has also opened its eyes on interdisplinary research. One of the institutional fruits that Europe could present would be the European Institute of Technology (EIT), which resembles M.I.T. in the U.S.. In Japan, as has been presented in regression model in the following part, compared to the U.S. case, environments for interdisplinary research has not reached a fruit bearing stage. Yet, it is noteworthy that the Japanese government's efforts to promote the interdisplinary fields are quite systematic. The first major policy example to be presented is the center of excellence (COE) project sponsored by the ministry of education, culture, sports, science and technology (MECSST). With the program, the ministry intends to develop a group of world class research teams throughout Japan. What is more eye-catching than just the framework of investment comes from the areas for investment. The program added interdisplinary fields, which covers from natural sciences and engineering to social sciences and humanities. In fact, various MECSST support programs have shown interdisplinary fields.

Chapter 6

Conclusion

1. Future for Communitarianism and liberalism

Theoretically it has been possible to distinguish different nations on a continuum of liberalism vs. communitarianism along different individual policy. This dichotomy is a purely theoretical one with an assumption that a tradition is a dominant component in a certain country. One interesting point to observe recently is a mixed trends of the two intellectual heritage in the policy settings not only in the U.S., but also in other countries. Another point is that depending on the level of government activities, the future expectation of communitarianism vs liberalism mix will be different.

First, in the U.S., on the historical legacy of

liberalism, there is a new transplant of communitarian ideas in different policy areas. It is possible to present two policy areas of such change. One is a recent welfare proposal by the Republican Party to introduce family responsibility for their elderly parents; it is to let the "able" grown -up children to pay their parents' nursing home bills. It is a change of thought from the past track, and even though it can be looked as a minimal change, it bears a seed for a communitarian idea. In Communitarian world view, the basic idea of constructing a community starts with an idea of network, in which family is an integral component. In this sense, welfare policy area would show a more communitarian component based on the existing one based on individualism.

My second example of policy idea change has been evidenced from the 1980s. The U.S. government, which has taken mainly the free economy principle from its early founding years, has begun to take a joint Research and development consortia efforts in the areas of semi conductor and electric car development. This policy pattern was a trade mark in Countries with a stronger communitarian policy tradition.

Despite this new introduction of communitarian ideas in the U.S. policy making settings, it is also noteworthy to mention that this new trend shows different degrees along state-local-federal levels. In my view, it is the local level and federal level where the new trends can affect most. In the local level, community network concept can actually and feasibly enhance the quality of life and policy effect in such areas as crime prevention and education. It is what Etzinoni and his colleagues are arguing for in the recent founding book for the rediscovery of communitarianism.

At the federal level, as I mentioned above, a meta policy change is possible. Federal government and Congress can set up a policy idea that can affect the local and state level policies. In relative terms, I argue that state government level would be less affected by the influx of communitarian ideas.

2. Policy Learning across nations and its policy implications

In the above paragraphs, I mentioned on the future of two policy ideas in different contexts. It would be meaningful to briefly mention what other countries would show in the future in order to draw out policy implications of the future changes. Even though one does not agree completely agree with the convergence theories and their off springs, people's values have been cross-affected. Together with more common physical environments and increasing reliance of societies on technology including A.I. technology, it would be a sensible forecasting to see policy convergence as well as ideas underlying the convergence.

Bibliography

Argyris, Chris., Personality and Organization, New York Harper, 1957

Argyris, Chris., Integrating the Individual and the Organization, New York. Routledge 2017 .

Albrow, Martin., Bureaucracy. Pall Mall Press. 1970.

Alford, Lionel Jr.(1999) "The Problem With Aviation Cots - commercial off the shelf purchasing", *Acquisition Review Quarterly*, Summer.

Alford, Lionel Jr. (2001) "The Problem with Aviation Cots", *IEEE Aerospace & electronics Systems Magazine* Febuary. pp.33-37.

Almond, Gabriel., "The Return to the State," American Political Science Review. vol 82. no.3. September 1988.

Amorelli, T. (1996) "Dual use and technology transfer in the titanium industry", IPTS Report 4, pp. 27–30.

Amsden, Alice Hoffenberg. Asia's next giant: South Korea and late industrialization. Oxford University Press, USA, 1992.

Anchordoguy, Marie. (1988) "Mastering the Market: Japanese Government Targeting of the Computer Industry", International organization, Volume 42, Issue 3. (Summer) pp.509-43. 1988.

Bellais, Renaud and Guichard, Renelle. (2006) "Defense

Innovation, technology transfers and Public Policy", *Defence and Peace Economics*, Volume 17, Number 3, June. pp. 273-286.

Bendix, Reinhard., Bureaucracy and the problem of power, in Robert merton ed. Reader in Bureaucracy. 1952.

Benguria, Gorka, Ana Belén , David Sellier, and Sandy Tay. (2002) "European COTS User Working Group: Analysis of the Common Problems and Current Practices of the European COTS Users", *Lecture Notes in Computer Science*, Volume 2255. pp.44-53.

Berelson, Bernard R., Paul F. Lazarsfeld, and William N. McPhee. Voting: A study of opinion formation in a presidential campaign. University of Chicago Press, 1954, 1986.

Berger, Suzanne. "Organizing interests in Western Europe: Pluralism, corporatism, and the transformation of politics." Cambridge University Press. 1983.

Berry, Jeffrey M. et al., The Rebirth of Urban Democracy, The Brookings Institution, Washington, D.C. 1993.

Blake, M.B. (2005) "Integrating large-scale group projects and software engineering approaches for early computer science courses", *IEEE Transactions on Education*, Feb. Volume: 48, Issue: 1. pp.63- 72.

Bo Rothstein, The crisis of the Swedish Social democrats and the future of the universal welfare state, Center for European Studies, March ,1992

Boltho, Andrea, and Barry Eichengreen. "The economic impact of European integration." 2008.

Boltho, A., & Glyn, A. "Can macroeconomic policies raise employment:, Int'l Lab. Rev. 134. 1995

Branscomb, Alic J., L., Brooks, H., Carter, A. and Epstein, G. (1992). *Beyond Spinoff: Military and Commercial Technologies in a Changing World*, Harvard Business School Press, Boston.

Brinton, Crane. The anatomy of revolution. 1938.

Brooks, Frederick. (1995) *The Mythical Man-Month*: Essays on Software Engineering, 20th Anniversary Edition, Addison-Wesley Professional, New York, NY.

Carr, R.K. (1994) "Doing technology transfer in federal laboratories", in: Suleiman, K. and Radosevich, R., Editors. *From Lab to Market. Commercialization of Public Sector Technology*, Plenum Press, New York, pp. 61–87

Charles Herzfeld. (2008) "How the change agent has changed", *Nature* 451, pp.403 - 404 (23 Jan)

Coch, Lester and J.R.P. French, " Overcoming Resistance to Change," Human Relations Vol. 1. 1948. pp.512-533.

Cowan, R. and Foray, D. (1995) "Quandaries in the economics of dual technologies and spillovers from military to civilian research and development", *Research Policy* 24, pp. 851–868.

Crozier, Michel. and Samuel Huntington, The Crisis of

Democracy Report on the Governability of Democracies to the Trilateral Commission., New York, New York University Press. 1975.

Dahl, Robert A., A Preface to Democratic Theory, Chicago, University of Chicago Press. 1956

Dahl, Robert A., Who Governs? New Haven Yale University Press 1961.

David Chandler. (2007) "Space: Dreams of the new space race", *Nature* 448, pp.988 - 991   August.

Demko, E.(1996) "Commercial-off-the shelf (COTS): a challenge to military equipment reliability", *Reliability and Mantainability Symposium*, 1996 Proceedings. "International Symposium on Product Quality and Integrity". Vol.: 22-25 Jan.   pp.7 - 12

Derthick, Martha, and Paul J. Quirk. The politics of deregulation. Brookings Institution Press, 2001

Diesing, Paul. How does social science work?: Reflections on practice. University of Pittsburgh Press, 1992.

Donald J. Reifer, Victor R. Basili, Barry W. Boehm and Betsy Clark. (2004) "COTS-Based Systems–Twelve Lessons Learned about Maintenance", Lecture Notes in Computer Science Volume 2959.

Easton, David., A Framework for Political Analysis, Prentice Hall. 1965.

Elias G. Carayannisa, , Everett M. Rogersb, Kazuo Kuriharac and Marcel M. Allbritton. (1998) "High-technology spin-offs from government R&D laboratories and research universities", *Technovation* Volume 18, Issue 1, January. pp. 1-11

Elmore, Richard., "Backward mapping: implementation research and policy decisions, political science quarterly, vol.94 number 4, winter 1979-1980

Etzinoi, Amitain.,The Spirit of Community : Rights, and The Communitarian Agenda. Crown Publishers, Inc. New York. 1993.

Evered. (2004) "Research in the behavioural and social sciences to improve cancer control and care: a strategy for development", *European Journal of Cancer* Volume 40, Issue 3 February pp.316-325.

Fong, Gwenda. (2004) "Adapting cots games for military simulation", VRCAI "04: *Proceedings of the 2004 ACM SIGGRAPH international conference on Virtual Reality continuum and its applications in industry.* June

Garvey, Gerald T., Peter L. Swan., "The economics of corporate governance: Beyond the Marshallian firm", Journal of Corporate Finance. Volume 1, Issue 2, August 1994

Gerschenkron, Alexander. (1962) Economic Backwardness in Historical Perspective: A Book ofEssays. Cambridge, MA: Harvard University Press.

Glass, Robert. (2002) *Facts and Fallacies of Software Engineering,* Addison-Wesley, New York, NY.

Goldthorpe, John H. The affluent worker in the class structure. Vol. 3. CUP Archive, 1969.

Gouldner, Alvin. Patterns of Industrial Bureaucracy, Free Press, Glencoe, IL, 1954.

Gourevitch, Peter. Politics in Hard Times: Comparative Responses to International Economic Crises. Ithaca and London, Cornell University Press. 1986

Hall, J. and Naff, R. (2000) "The cost of COTS" Digital Avionics Systems Conferences, Proceedings, October. 7th-13th. Volume: 1, pp. 4B1/ 1-4B1/6. Philadelphia, PA, USA.

Hall, Peter. Governing the Economy: The Politics of State Intervention in Britain and France, oxford University Press. 1986.

Hobbes, Thomas. *Leviathan,* Penguin Classics, 1992

James, Andrew. (2006) "US Defence R&D Spending: An Analysis of the Impacts",

Huntington, Samuel P. "The Democratic Distemper," Public Interest, no.41. Fall, 1975

Immergut, Ellen M. Health politics: interests and institutions in Western Europe. CUP Archive, 1992.

James, Andrew. (2006) "The transatlantic defence R&D gap: causes, consequences and controversies", *Defence and Peace Economics,* Vol.17, No.3, 2006: pp. 223-238.

James, Andrew, Cox, D and Rigby, J. (2005) "Testing the boundaries of Public-Private Partnership: the privatisation of the UK Defence Evaluation & Research Agency", *Science & Public Policy*, 32 (2), April: pp.155-161.

Janis, Irving L. "Groupthink." IEEE Engineering Management Review 36.1 (2008): 36.

Janis, Irving L. Victims of Group Think 1973.

Janis, Irving. Groupthink. In E. Griffin (Ed.) A First Look at Communication Theory (pp. 235 - 246). New York: McGrawHill. 1991.

Joint Committee on Western Europe. Order and conflict in contemporary capitalism. Ed. John H. Goldthorpe. Oxford: Clarendon Press, 1984.

Katzenstein, Peter. Between Power and Plenty, The University of Wisconsin Press. 1978.

Kaufman, Herbert."Emerging Conflicts in the Doctrines of Public Administration," American Political Science Review, vol 50. no 4. Summer 1956.

Kim, Junmo. (2007)a "Will Technology Fusion induce the Paradigm Change of University Education?" International Journal of Technology Management (IJTM) Vol. 38., no.3. pp.220-234.

Kim, Junmo. (2007)b *Policy Alternatives to promote interdisplinary academic and educational design* Report to the Presidential Advisory Council on Science & Technology (PACST), (March 2007- May 2007)

Kim, Junmo. (2002) "Network building between research institutions and small & medium enterprises(SMEs):

dynamics of innovation network building and implications for a policy option", *International Journal of Technology, Policy and Management* (IJTPM) Vol. 2. No.3. Winter. pp.272-285.

Klimek, Peter, Rudolf Hanel, and Stefan Thurner. "Parkinson's Law quantified: three investigations on bureaucratic inefficiency." Journal of Statistical Mechanics: Theory and Experiment 2009.03 (2009)

Kline, Ronald R. and Thomas C. Lassman. (2005) "Competing Research Traditions in American Industry: Uncertain Alliances between Engineering and Science at Westinghouse Electric, 1886–1935", Journal : Enterprise Soc., Dec. vol.6. pp.601 - 645

Kuhn, Thomas. (1962) *The Structure of Scientific Revolutions*, The Chicago University Press.

Lewin, Kurt.,"Group Decisions and Social Change," In G.E. Swanson, T.M. Newcomb and E.L. Hartley, eds. Readings in Social Psychology, New York, Holt. 1952.

Li, Jingyue, Finn Olav Bjørnson, Reidar Conradi and Vigdis B. Kampenes. (2006) "An empirical study of variations in COTS-based software development processes in the Norwegian IT industry", *Empirical Software Engineering* Volume 11, Number 3 September.

Lindblom, Charles E., The Intelligence of Democracy: Decision through Mutual Adjustment. The Free Press New York. Collier-Macmillan Limited. 1965.

Lipset, Seymour Martin, Martin A. Trow, and James S. Coleman, Union Democracy: The Internal Politics of the International Typographical Union. The Free Press. Glencoe, Illinois. 1956.

Lipsky, M., Street Level Bureaucracy: Street-Level Bureaucracy, 30th Anniversary Edition: Dilemmas of the individual in Public Services Russel Sage Foundation. New York 2010.

Locke, John. The second treatise of civil government. Broadview Press, 2015.

Lodge, Martin. (ed.) et al., The Oxford Handbook of Classics in Public Policy and Administration. Oxford University Press 2016.

Lowi, Theodore., The End of Liberalism: The Second Republic of the United States. Second edition. W.W. Norton & Company. New York and London. 1979

Madison, James. "Federalist paper number 10." The Federalist Papers (1787): 23-33

March, James G. "Bounded rationality, ambiguity, and the engineering of choice." The bell journal of economics (1978): 587-608.

March, James G. and Johan P. Olsen. Rediscovering Institutions: The Organizational Basis of Politics. Free Press. London and New York. 1995.

McGraw, G. and J. Viega. (1999) "Why COTS Software Increases Security Risks" ICSE Workshop on Testing

Distributed Component-Based Systems, May 1999.

Merton, Robert., Ailsa P.Gray, Barbara Hockey, Hanan C.Selvin, Reader in Bureaucracy 1952.

Mills, C Wright., Power Elite. New York Oxford University Press 1956.

Molas-Gallart, Jordi. (1997) "Which way to go? Defence technology and the diversity of 'dual-use' technology transfer", *Research Policy* Volume 26, Issue 3, October 1997, pp. 367-385.

Morone, James A. The Democratic Wish: Popular Participation and the Limits of American Government. Basic Books, A Division of Harper and Collins Publishers.1990.,

North, Douglas,Institutions, Institutional Change, and Economic Performance, Cambridge University Press. 1990.

O'Connor, James., The Fiscal Crisis of the State New York. ST. Martin's Press. 1973

Olson, Mancur., The Logic of Collective Action: Public Goods and the Theory of Groups, Harvard University Press, 1965.

Olson, Mancur., The Rise and Fall of Nations: Economic Growth, Stagflation, and Social Rigidities. Yale University Press New Haven and London. 1982.

Ostrom, Elinor. Governing the Commons: The Evolution of Institutions for Collective Action. Cambridge university press, 1990.

Parsons, Talcott. Politics and Social Structure The Free Press. New York. 1969.

Pateman,Carole., Participation and Democratic Theory, Cambridge University Press, 1970

Philip, K. L., K. Backett-Milburn, S. Cunningham-Burley, and J. B. Davis. (2003) "Practicing what we preach? A practical approach to bringing research, policy and practice together in relation to children and health inequalities", Health Education Research., Oct. vol.18, pp.568 - 579.

Pizzorno. Alessandro,"Interests and parties in pluralism." Organizing interests in Western Europe. Cambridge University Press. 1981.

Polsby, Nelson., Community Power and Political Theory, New Haven Yale University Press. 1963.

Pressman, Jeffrey L., and Aaron Wildavsky. Implementation: How great expectations in Washington are dashed in Oakland; Or, why it's amazing that federal programs work at all, this being a saga of the Economic Development Administration as told by two sympathetic observers who seek to build morals on a foundation. Vol. 708. Univ of California Press, 1984.

Putnam, Robert., Making Democracy Work: Civic Traditions in Modern Italy Princeton University Press. 2001.

Quackenbush, Stephen. "The Rationality of Rational Choice

Theory", Empirical and Theoretical Research in International RelationsVolume 30, 2004 - Issue 2

Rosenberg, Hans., Bureaucracy, Aristocracy, and Autocracy: The Prussian Experience 1660-1815. Cambridge, Massachusetts. Harvard University Press. 1958.

Sapolsky, Harvey M.(1992) *Comparing Health and Defense.* MIT Center for International Studies (CIS), Cambridge, September.

Satori, Giovanni., Democratic Theory Detroit, Wayne State University Press 1962

Schattschneider, Elmer E. "I960. The semi-sovereign people." A Realist View of Democracy in America. The Dryden Press, 1968.

Schumpeter, Joseph A. Capitalism, Socialism, and Democracy. Harper Torchbooks. 1942, 1947

Sharon Weinberger. (2008) "Defense research: Still in the lead?", *News@Nature* 451, pp.390 - 393 (23 Jan)

Skocpol, Theda. State and Social Revolution: A Comparative Analysis of France, Russia, and China. Cambridge University Press. 1979.

Skocpol, Theda. "Bringing the State Back In: Retrospect and Prospect", The 2007 Johan Skytte Prize Lecture. Scandinavian Political Studies, Volume31, Issue2, May 2008. Pages 109-124

Solow, Robert. (1956) "A Contribution to the Theory of Economic Growth", *The Quarterly Journal of Economics,*

70(1), 65-94.

Skocpol, Theda. "Bringing the State Back In: Retrospect and Prospect", The 2007 Johan Skytte Prize Lecture. Scandinavian Political Studies, Volume31, Issue2, May 2008. Pages 109-124

Steinmo, Sven. et al. ed., Structuring Politics: Historical Institutionalism in Comparative Analysis Cambridge University Press 1992.

Stowsky, Jay. (1996) "The dual-use dilemma: technologies for commercial and military applications", *Issues in Science and Technology* Vol.13, Issue no.2. National Academy of Sciences, pp.56-64.

Stowsky, Jay. (1992) "From Spin-off to Spin-On: Redefining the Military's Role in American Technological Development," in Wayne Sandholtz et al, *The Highest Stakes*: The Economic Foundations of the Next Security System. New York, Oxford University Press, pp. 114-140

Taylor, Michael, and Douglas Rae. "An analysis of crosscutting between political cleavages." Comparative Politics 1.4 (1969): 534-547.

Thelen, Kathleen. "Regulating Uber: The Politics of the Platform Economy in Europe and the United States" 23 November 2018 Perspectives on Politics. Volume 16 Issue 4 (Published online by Cambridge University Press)

Thompson, Victor A. Modern organization. University of

Alabama Press, 1977.

Thompson, James D. Organizations in action: Social science bases of administrative theory. Routledge, 2017.

Thompson, James D. "Theory and Research in Administration." (1967): 691-694.

Tocqueville, Alexis de. "Democracy in America." Democracy: A Reader. Columbia University Press, 2016. 67-76.

Voas, J. (1998)a "A Defensive Approach to Testing Systems that Contain COTS and Third-Party Functionality In the Proceedings AQUIS '98, Venice, April 1998

Voas, J. (1998)b. "COTS software: The economical choice?", *IEEE Software*, vol. 15, no.2. pp.16 -19.

Wade, Robert. Governing the market: Economic theory and the role of government in East Asian industrialization. Princeton University Press, 2004.

Winter, Don C. (1996) "Modular, Reusable FlightSoftware For Production Aircraft", 15thAIAA/IEEEDigital Avionics Systems Conference Proceedings, October, pp. 401-406.

Inside higher education "Institutionalizing' Interdisciplinary Research" July 25th, 2007

Military & Aerospace Electronics Magazine, "COTS integration and acquisition is focus of Military & Aerospace Electronics Forum", , January 2008 internet ed.

Military & Aerospace Electronics Magazine, "French and Australian navies use Thales PowerPC boards for mine hunting", March, 2001. internet ed.

Theoretical Perspectives for the Public Sector and Its Agendas

초판발행 2023년 10월 10일
지 은 이 김준모
펴 낸 이 김복환
펴 낸 곳 도서출판 지식나무
등록번호 제301-2014-078호
주   소 서울시 중구 수표로12길 24
전   화 02-2264-2305(010-6732-6006)
팩   스 02-2267-2833
이 메 일 booksesang@hanmail.net

ISBN 979-11-87170-56-3
값 15,000원